MW01632251

# THE TIRE MOM

## My Highway to Healing

To: Neal and family,
Thank you for all the wonderful content that you are producing ♡

# THE TIRE MOM

## My Highway to Healing

Stay safe!
Diana Hubner

DIANA HUBNER

WITH NANCY RUE

Tire Mom

Rochester, NY

Published by The Tire Mom LLC, Rochester, NY



Interior graphics by M. Brandon Silva
Cover design and layout by Nina Alvarez
The Tire Mom, LLC logo by Athens Aikman

For permission to reprint portions of this book, or to order a review copy, contact: diana@thetiremom.com

Visit TheTireMom.com to learn more.

ISBN-13: 978-0-578-58036-4

# Disclaimer

The views and opinions expressed in this publication are those of the author and do not necessarily represent the position of any other individual, company, organization, or agency. While the author has gathered information from multiple sources, the author is not an expert, and the information in this publication should not be considered professional advice. The events and conversations in this book are based on the author's present recollection of them. Some names and identifying characteristics have been changed to protect the privacy of individuals. Although the author and publisher have made every effort to make this book as complete and accurate as possible, the author and publisher do not assume responsibility or liability for any errors or omissions in the content of this publication. All information is provided "AS IS" with no guarantee of accuracy, completeness, or correctness, and with no warranties of any kind, express or implied.

To Clayton—my Mr. Darcy—and
the wonderful children
we raised together.

I will see you again,
just not yet.

# CONTENTS

## The Tire Mom Mission Statement

To make the USA a safer place by educating people on how to read the manufacture date on their tires.

Please visit TheTireMom.com to read the state-by-state chronicle of The Tire Mom's first U.S. tour gifting fifty new sets of tires in fifty states, as well as the second U.S. tour in which she shared her memoir *The Tire Mom: My Highway to Healing* along with life-saving information she learned from tire experts on the first tour.

Connect with The Tire Mom on instagram @thetiremom and on twitter @momtire

## How to Find Your Tire Identification Number

All tires have an abundance of information printed on the sidewall but you must know how to find and interpret it. Tires have the letters DOT printed on them, followed by a series of numbers and letters indicating the manufacturing facility code, the tire size code, the manufacturer identity number, and finally, four numbers officially called the "tire identification number" (but what The Tire Mom affectionately named the "Tire Halo") that indicate the week and year the tire was made. For instance, a Tire Halo containing "2519" means that the tire was made in the 25th week of 2019. The diagram to the right can help you find the Tire Halo on your own tires.

# FINDING YOUR TIRE HALO

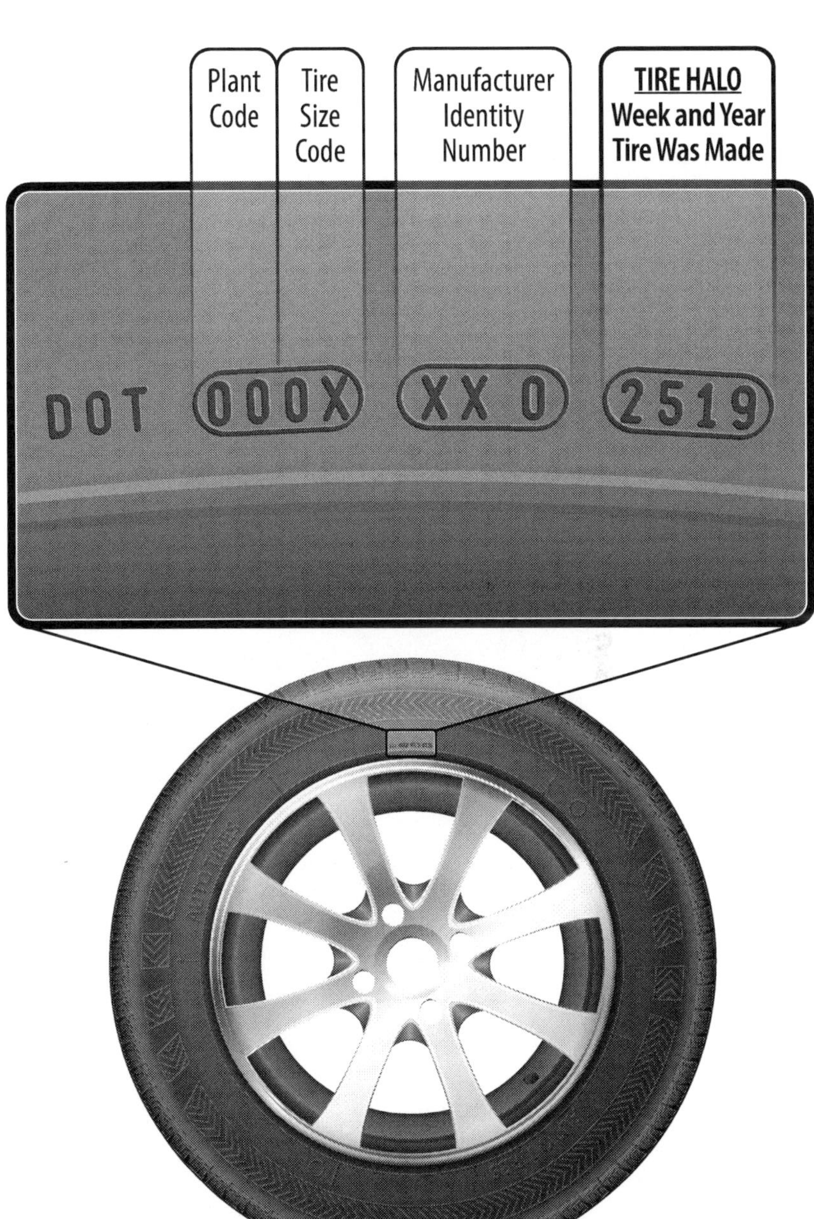

# FOREWORD

One of the greatest lessons I remember Dr. Clayton Hubner emphasizing to us as students in Hawaii was sustainability. His college class on leadership in business was actually the first time I'd heard the term. This lecture had a deliverable attached to it to create something that would last forever. It was a mind-numbing assignment, but even years later, it changed the way I think and do everything today. He taught us how to create a legacy.

***Legacy through empowering others was Clayton's method of influence***—and it's felt today throughout the world in over seventy countries.

He was always talking about his kids. Every class he seemed to share something about each of his kids. Somehow, he always wove in a story about his family—I think as a way to help us remember that even with all the things we were learning, family is what mattered. The way he taught students, worked on projects, and loved his family was built to last. We loved it. The way he taught made me feel like I could create a home and future where work and family could blend joyfully, happily, as he had done.

I remember him speaking in class so proudly of his wife who was working on a clothing company. This was when the Internet was super clunky and hard to navigate—before Facebook moved to the public eye, before YouTube and Instagram even existed. He shared how Diana was able to find companies in India to manufacture products, how she did quality control, how she was creating a brand, and how she made her first sales.

More importantly, love for his wife felt tangible through his stories of her. I learned that business is about family, relationships, and the impact we make on others in the universe, which also applies to the individuals that matter most to us—in our families, communities, churches. It was cool how he used Diana's ingenuity in her personal international business ventures to teach us how we could also become entrepreneurs while maintaining focus on family, relationships, and love for others.

***Love was Clayton's method of teaching.***

Personally, he spent countless hours with me in his office. He mentored me for years and years. He told stories. He asked about my hopes and dreams. He surprisingly had an incredible insight on almost every topic in the most random subjects. He coached me through my first venture. Without me even asking, he put his name on the line for me with a decision maker at a company to get me my first major consulting job.

He had my back. Since then, that path he helped me get to has taken me worldwide as a consultant to over a hundred companies! This man changed my life and I only pray I am using the lessons he taught me wisely to create sustainable projects that empower others.

Years later, even after I'd graduated and lived in different states, he would call me just to chat and share his thoughts on global topics and opportunities he saw coming in the future.

A true mentor. A true friend. A rare type of wonderful.

If you were to speak with those associated with Clayton, you'd find that my experience with him isn't unique. His vision caught the imagination of all he associated with. A genius. A light. A humble yet powerful man with intercultural sensitivity and international impact. A man filled with *aloha*.

Clayton created environments of high trust, high inspiration, and high implementation to lift others and influence the world for good.

***Lifting others was Clayton's method of delivery.***

This book will inspire you to live a better life and perhaps save your life (literally) in the process. Read this book to do great things!

As Diana would say:

> *All of us are supposed to take risks in life. If we have plans but never leave the house, we will not accomplish great things.*

*Aloha,*

Richie Norton, award-winning bestselling author of *The Power of Starting Something Stupid: How to Crush Fear, Make Dreams Happen, and Live Without Regret*

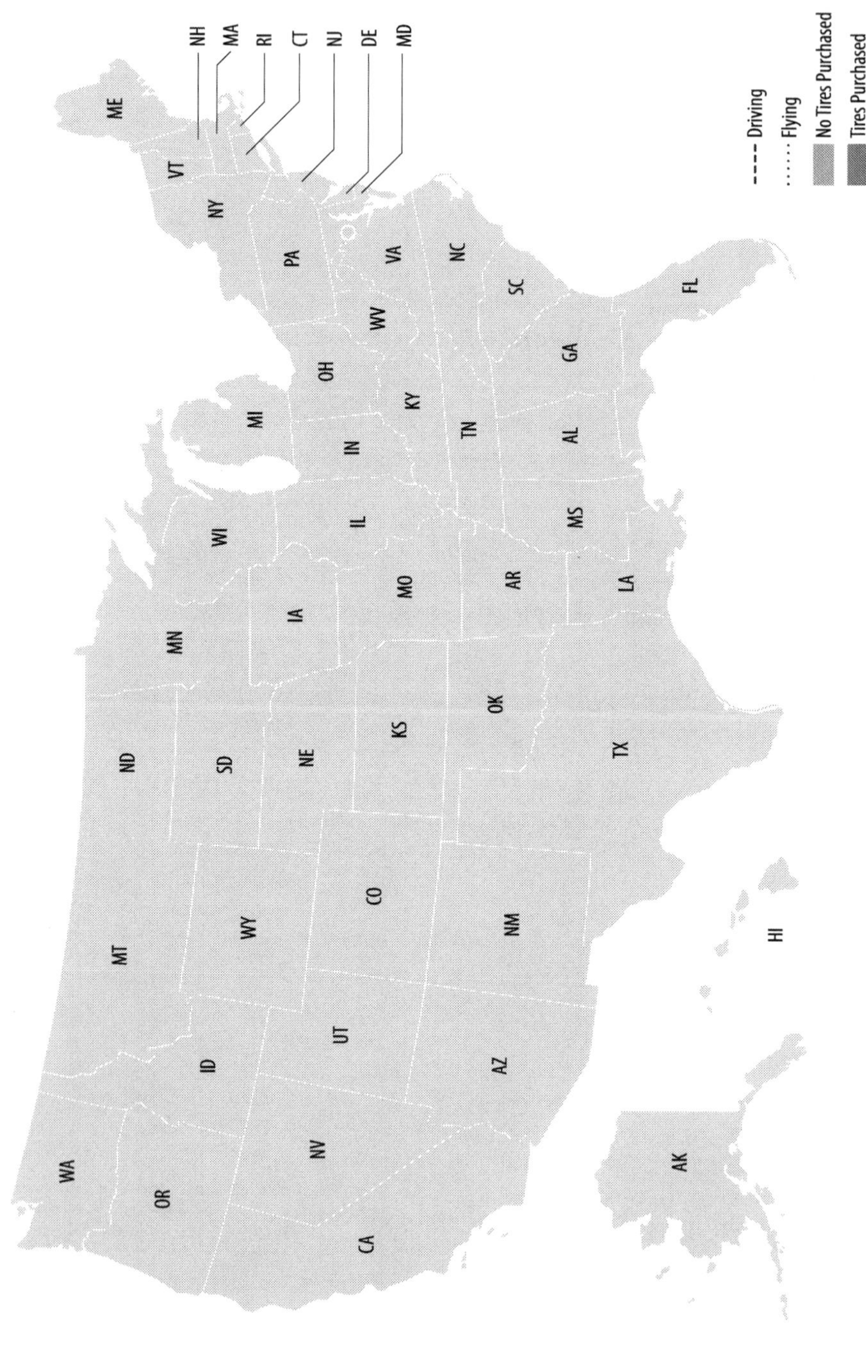


THE TIRE MOM JOURNEY
*January 2018*

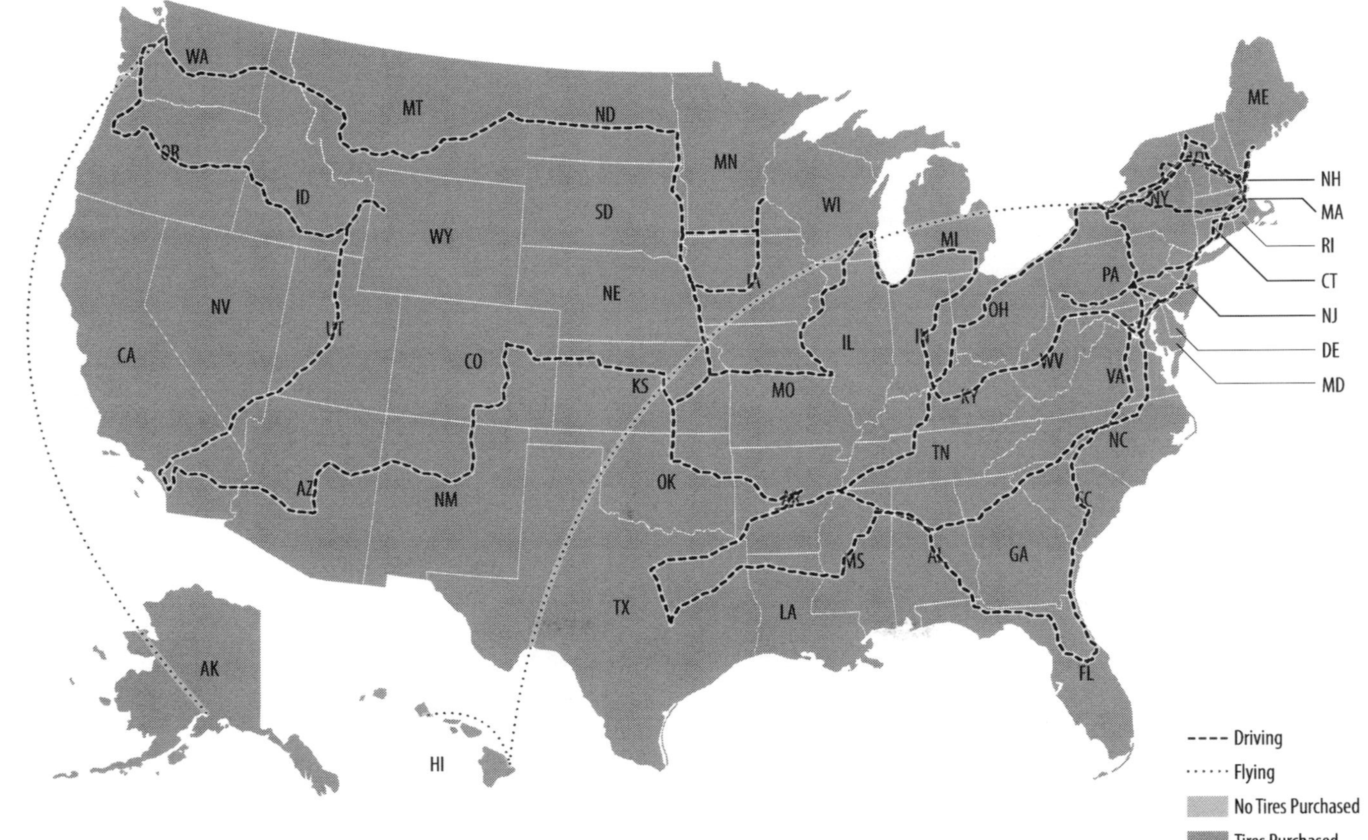


THE TIRE MOM JOURNEY

*December 2018*

# INTRODUCTION

When I walked into the tire store that day in 2012, I was on high alert. I was only there to pick up my pre-owned Suburban with its set of four new tires. Not a big deal, right? But, in fact, it was.

By the time I got to the counter, the tire technician looked up at me expectantly.

"Hubner," I said. "The Suburban?"

"It's ready," he said and slid the receipt toward me with my keys.

I drew in a breath. "What is the DOT date on these tires?"

The tire technician took a step back. It was clear from his baffled expression that he had not been expecting that. He recovered nicely though, and pointed to a spot on the receipt.

"Says here they were all made in 2012."

I simply said "thank you" and turned toward the exit. I was on a mission.

I was slightly relieved that one hurdle had been overcome but was still bracing myself for the next step: checking the dates on the sides of my tires to be sure they matched the dates on the receipt.

I was marching toward my Suburban when I heard a male voice behind me.

"Ma'am? Ma'am?"

The voice wasn't familiar, and there was no reason why it should be. I was in Virginia where I barely knew anyone. I turned and saw a well-dressed man, a little shorter than I am—which isn't unusual since I'm almost six feet tall—and something about his manner told me he was well-educated.

"Excuse me," he said, seeming intrigued. "I have never heard a woman ask about the DOT date on a tire." He gave a slight shrug. "How do you know about DOT dates?" He wasn't at all condescending. In fact, there was a hint of camaraderie in his voice.

Still, I hesitated to answer him for two reasons. One, my feelings were very real and very raw. If I explained that to him, I might cry in front of this complete stranger. Two, I wasn't sure he'd handle it well. Few people did.

I decided to confirm if he was just curious or if it was worth going into more detail. "Do you really want to know the reason?" I asked.

"Yes," he said.

He seemed genuinely interested so I took another deep breath. "*Not* knowing that vital information about tires contributed to the accident that killed my husband on June 17 of this year, Father's Day."

I was right to have hesitated. The man's face showed a mixture of shock and dismay. I could see pain in his eyes as he shook his head.

"I am so sorry," he said.

I watched as he walked away, still shaking his bowed head. By then tears had welled up in my eyes, and I found myself breathing hard so I wouldn't burst into sobs there in the parking lot.

After all, it had only been two months.

Whenever something like this happens, I always flash back to the horrific moment when my world disintegrated.

I was on vacation at our home in New York while my fifty-three-year-old husband, Clayton, was finishing teaching spring term at Brigham Young University–Hawaii. The two youngest of our five children were with me, as well as Clayton's parents, and despite the fact that the rest of the family was spread all over the globe, it was a good season in our lives. Basically, at fifty-two, I had everything in my life that I wanted.

We were living in Hawaii on the island of Oahu. Clayton was the love of my life—my lover and protector. We lived somewhat cramped in a three-bedroom duplex with the kids who were still at home and five dogs, but hey, we were living in Hawaii. I worked as a substitute teacher at the elementary school helping children with math and reading. Every three years, we took the whole family on a vacation to the mainland USA to do road trips, which had brought me to New York. Life was very good, and I felt blessed.

Naturally there were challenges. I was trying to downsize and pack up our New York home. But it weighs on me now that I thought that was stress. I had no idea what stress was.

Until that Father's Day in 2012, when the phone rang.

I still had an old flip phone, so there was no way to know who it was until I answered. When I got a call on a Sunday, it was usually someone in the family with something funny to tell me.

However, the voice on the other end was professional and the concerned tone of his voice immediately put me on guard. He verified my identity then said, "Mrs. Hubner, are you driving?"

What an odd question. "No. I'm sitting in my bedroom writing my daughter a letter."

I heard him take a breath, and I went from apprehensive to fearful in a millisecond.

His exact words escape me. They really don't matter. The message would have been just as life-destroying no matter how he said it.

Basically, he told me my husband, my beloved Clayton, was dead. Killed in an automobile accident.

I've learned since then that the most common reaction to such devastating news is disbelief, and I was no exception. I hit him with a barrage of questions:

"Who are you?"

"Where are you?"

"Give me the phone number you're calling from!"

At first he simply exhaled, as if he were waiting for the news to sink in. But I couldn't let it. This couldn't be true. Clayton and I had so much more to do in our lives. He was my everything. I thought we would grow old together and travel the world. We had so many plans and dreams—and they had been shattered in that single instant.

The only image I can use to describe my life at that moment is that of a glass ball thrown onto a concrete driveway with devastating force. My life was now those hundreds of shards of glass.

Somehow one of those shattered pieces of myself wrote down his name and phone number.

When we hung up, my body became rigid, my breathing short and fast. To say that my mind was racing is an understatement.

I wanted to understand, but I didn't.

I wanted to know the horrific truth, but I didn't want to accept it.

The only thing that got me up and moving was the sole responsibility for my family that now rested on my shoulders.

My family members were scattered across the world, and somehow I needed to reach them, but I had no idea how to share such overwhelming news. I don't remember who I called or how I contacted people, but with the help of family and friends, I somehow managed to do what was necessary.

I then spent a sleepless night packing our bags for Colorado, where Clayton's body was in a morgue, awaiting transfer to a funeral home. By the time we arrived, I felt as though a sheet of bubble wrap had been pulled over my entire body. I could see, hear, and even understand what was going on around me, but I was in a distant surreal realm of comforting numbness.

Somehow, I managed to process the information that my mother's truck, which Clayton had borrowed for a ten-day road trip, had two fourteen-year-old tires and two new tires. The tread on one of the old tires had come off and the truck had swerved to the right, off the freeway, and rolled three times—throwing Clayton from the truck.

I didn't fully comprehend that information then. I was doing what I'm sure thousands of grieving widows have done—I was focusing on the things I could control. Clayton was always frugal, very good with our money, but regardless of that, I wanted him to be cremated in a nice white shirt. He didn't have one in his luggage, and instead of going to the usual thrift store (our default shopping destination), I went into a men's department store and paid seventy dollars for the nicest, whitest shirt I could find.

As I was walking out of the store, it was as though Clayton was walking beside me, shaking his head in frustration. *Really? Seventy dollars for a shirt I'm going to be CREMATED in?*

*Look,* I said in my mind, *if you don't want me spending that kind of money on your shirt then you just come back here and fix this yourself. I am GETTING you a nice SHIRT!*

When I was finally able to see Clayton at the funeral home, I was still wrapped in bubble wrap and barely noticed the newness of his shirt. All I saw was my husband, appearing to be asleep except that there was no rise and fall of his breathing. Oddly, at that moment, I remembered a documentary about John F. Kennedy. When Jackie saw him in his coffin, she asked one of the bodyguards for scissors, and she cut some locks of his hair.

"Does anyone have any scissors?" I asked.

Aunt Frankie produced her Swiss Army knife, which included scissors. I tenderly put my hand on Clayton's head . . . his hair had grown since the last time I'd cut it. I cut a few locks of hair from different places on his head and slipped the locks into the red velvet bag the funeral director had given me containing Clayton's wedding band. With my hand in the bag, I could feel that the ring was no longer round. It too had suffered in the accident.

I was able to take Clayton's ashes home with me—white shirt and all. I was amazed at the weight of them. The box was mahogany with mountains etched into it, and I had to carry a special certificate to go through the scanners at the security checkpoint. Somehow that made him seem still alive.

But he was definitely not. As we flew back to Rochester, I cried silently as two of my children slept and I looked out the window of the plane. The clouds flying by were beautiful in their variations of color and shape. In my head I knew God loved me, but when I tried to reconcile this with the reality of what I was going through, I could only let the tears run down my face.

This was not how my life was supposed to be. Clayton and I had many plans for our future. We both loved to travel and we both had a great love for the outdoors, road trips, and national parks. We had lived in seven different states in the US and in two foreign countries, which meant we had moved twelve times in our twenty-seven years of marriage. Everywhere we went, we loved going for walks on the beach or hikes in the woods. We loved watching movies and playing family games. We loved working on projects around the house and making things together. We loved our life and our children.

How was I going to live without him?

After the second memorial service in Laie, Hawaii,

I turned my heart off. I had to think with my head, and looming ahead of me were huge mountains of decisions to climb. I couldn't just stay in bed and cry for days. I had to take care of that family Clayton and I loved so much. I kept the bubble wrap around me for a while.

But when the bubble wrap gave out, I gave out. What else can you do with a smashed heart, with the hard and unrelenting burden of grief? For three years, I was a robot. I focused on the task in front of me, the next decision that had to be made. It was the only way I could think of to make the pain stop.

I didn't find the real way to heal my pain, the lasting way to peace, for quite a while. That is the story that will be told in the pages that follow. What I want you to know now is that the mission I eventually went on was in large part to prevent others from experiencing the heartache from accidents like Clayton's. I feel that if I can empower people with the knowledge I didn't have before the accident, it can help to continue healing the pain still in my heart.

It all began with learning about tires.

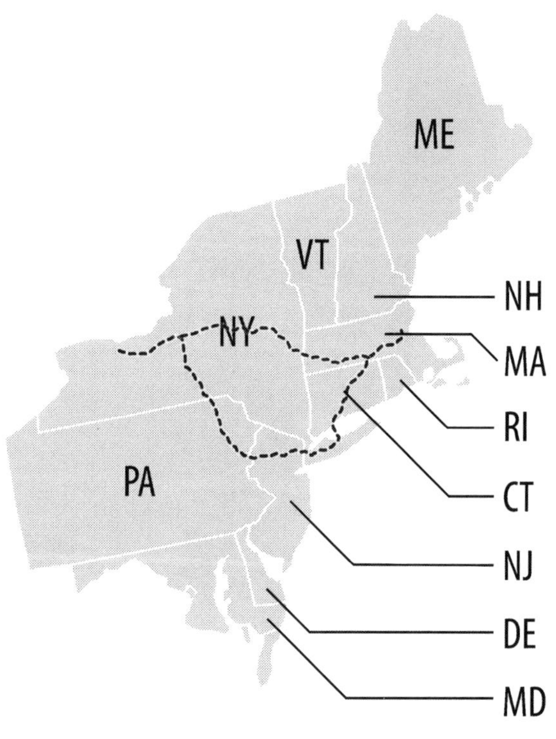


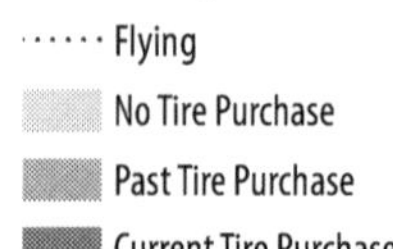


MAIDEN VOYAGE

*October 24-29, 2017 (6 days)*

# CHAPTER ONE

## THE BIRTH OF AN IDEA

Several years after Clayton died, I needed to reach a friend on the phone. I can't recall now what I needed, but I know it felt urgent at the time. Most things did. My friend's husband answered the phone, but when I asked him if he'd put her on, there was a pause, one of those pregnant pauses.

"You know what, Diana?" he said. "You only call when you need something."

No, it wasn't delivered gently by any means, but it wasn't an accusation either. Just a straightforward statement. And it was true.

Let me just say two things at this point. First, the anger stage of grief is very real. In my continuous low-level fury, I tended to just blurt things out, even when it came to asking for help. Second, I will be the first to admit that I've never been one to shy away from speaking my mind, but Clayton was gifted at diplomatically dealing with people, including me. That would account for many people's surprise when, in my grief, I didn't filter my speech the way my late husband would have.

I knew that what my friend's husband had said was true. I slumped where I stood. Oh, man. He was not the first person I'd inadvertently offended as I muddled my way through. This man had touched on a truth about how I'd chosen to cope with Clayton's death: always just focusing on the next task that had to be done: downsizing the house in Hawaii, shipping belongings hither and yon, and handling logistics for my five children, one of whom was across the world in New Caledonia.

As Anne Morrow Lindbergh wrote in her wonderful little book *Gift from the Sea:*

> *To be a woman is to have interests and duties, raying out in all directions from the central mother-core, like spokes from the hub of a wheel. The pattern of our lives is essentially circular. We must be open to all points of the compass: husband, children, friends, home, community; stretched out, exposed, sensitive like a spider's web to each breeze that blows, to each call that comes.*[1]

Truly, emotional survival and the physical safety of my family had become more important than developing and maintaining meaningful relationships outside the family. That phone conversation became a turning point

---

1 Anne Morrow Lindbergh, *Gift from the Sea* (New York: Pantheon Books, 2005), 22.

for me. I knew I needed to switch my emotions back on and open my heart to connecting with the wonderful people around me. I was deeply saddened that the hard, negative side of my grief had spilled over onto other people, and I didn't want to keep making that mistake.

I had to move forward.

The question, of course, was *how?* I had heard that out of the top five life stressors, I was experiencing two simultaneously: the death of a loved one and moving, which I had done three times in two years. I knew the healing process would be complex and was not one I could go through without help. Now the question was: *Who could help me move forward?* The people close to me couldn't be objective—and I did not want to burden them. They had already helped me so much. I wanted someone I could be vulnerable with. Someone professional who believed in God. I didn't just want secular wisdom. I wanted guidance on a spiritual level.

I wasn't unfamiliar with therapy. Clayton and I had sought counseling at times in our marriage. We were two very different and strong personalities, and we needed assistance in developing our skills to work together as a team. So my first step was to get recommendations from people I knew, which led me to a wonderful therapist.

We always started our sessions with prayer. He listened and helped me identify hidden emotions and issues to work through and refine my skills in my new role as a single parent. This healing process has taken longer than I expected, but it has been worth it.

This process helped me realize things in my everyday life. At one point, I was upset with my seventeen-year-old son for something he'd done and was telling him what the consequences for his actions would be. He interrupted me, and I'll never forget what he said:

"Mama, don't try to discipline me like Papa. Discipline me like you."

He was absolutely right. The problem was I had been so intertwined with Clayton, I didn't know who I was without him. Losing a spouse really is an identity crisis. I had no idea in those early days that seeking to find myself was going to be so key in moving forward with my life.

By the time I started therapy, I was living in Rochester, New York, back in the house Clayton and I had intended to sell before the accident happened. I had been in therapy several years by the time my kids had all finished high school and my mother, who had been living with me for two years, had died of a stroke. I was in a state of transition as well as additional grief with the passing of my mother. What to do now?

I had long felt a strong motivation to write a book to tell my story but felt both a fundamental lack of access to my own feelings and a great sense of inadequacy in expressing myself. At the age of two, I had experienced a stroke that temporarily paralyzed my left side. Our doctor, assuming I had a brain tumor (which ended up not being the case), recommended that I be allowed to play and be active to restore my natural growth and development. Though I continued to walk with a slight limp for a year, this "treatment," along with a diagnosis of dyslexia in early elementary school, led to an emphasis on physical activity and a de-emphasis on academic achievement. So school and especially writing did not come naturally to me. This led me to internalize a sense of being a "damaged" child, which continued to inform how I felt about myself as an adult. In my vulnerable emotional state in the years following Clayton's death, I just could not imagine exposing myself, and my weaknesses, to the world. But I still had a desire to help others by sharing my story.

It seemed that one way I could begin to gain the confidence and skills I needed to fulfill that dream would be to go back to school. I was more than ready to take on the challenge of chipping away at the deeply rooted less-than-desirable label of a girl who didn't know how to write. My idea was to enroll in a writing class at Monroe Community College (MCC) in Rochester, New York, and as an initial step, I had to send the school my college transcripts so they could evaluate my eligibility. They wrote back saying that they could not accept my transcripts because they were more than three years old. And indeed they were—by a factor of ten. With my academic past officially obliterated, I'd have to start from scratch and take the pretests MCC required to enroll in the writing and math classes I desired to attend.

This setback left me feeling discouraged and uncertain about this path. When I received that response from the college, I was stunned. I'd never heard of there being a statute of limitations on my prior course credit, and all I could think was:

*Really?*

*Ground zero?*

*I now have to study in order to even pass the pretests before I am even allowed to take the math and writing classes?*

I had been prepared to take a step up, and instead I was being forced to take ten steps back. It felt a lot like falling down. I asked myself some hard questions. Was this really where I needed to go? Did I have to rearrange my schedule to include study time in preparation for the pretests, which covered basic subjects I wasn't even interested in?

Ever since the accident, it seemed to be a recurring theme: trying to move forward but getting redirected. And often the answer, after being redirected, was to simply make the next mental, emotional, or physical mini-move and see what happened.

And at that time, that meant cleaning out the garage. Our home in Rochester had essentially become our storage area while we lived in Hawaii. Clayton and I had actually built a wall down the center of the two-door garage specifically to create storage, and over time, every last millimeter of space had been filled with our stuff. Looking at this was overwhelming. This would be a mammoth undertaking.

Since Clayton's death, I had avoided that side of the garage. I knew there were things in all those boxes that I needed, like tools, but I couldn't bring myself to open the door because I didn't want to confront the memories and rediscover the life I had lost. I think I felt in a way that if I hung on to all of the stuff that represented my life with my husband, I could also hang on to my life with him. I was unwilling to confront my feelings just like I was unwilling to confront the pile of stuff in my garage—and it was time to open both of them up and find the tools I needed to move forward in my life.

Still, when my daughter Camilla and I opened the garage door, let's just say that daunting and overwhelming don't even begin to describe how we felt about the task that stood before us.

But we did it in five weeks: two huge garage sales, ten trips to donation centers, and two trips to the recycling center. The day when we could finally touch the back wall was nothing short of momentous. Without Camilla's help, the weight of that task might have crushed me, but with her, I was able to accomplish a significant step toward lifting a burden I had long carried and clearing some headspace to begin healing.

I was learning a lot about being willing to receive help.

As a reward, Camilla and I indulged our mutual love of the outdoors by camping at the Adirondack Loj (Lodge) at Heart Lake, New York, where we had been many times when Clayton was alive. We did things we had not done before: we rented a canoe and paddleboard and swam at Heart Lake. We volunteered at Seneca Lake Camp for a week, which meant sleeping out in the woods, helping with the different programs, and letting nature be our classroom. It was wonderful to be *out*. Just being in the wilderness is in and of itself freeing.

But two weeks after returning from Seneca Lake Camp in August 2017, I woke up at 1:30 a.m. with a temperature of 103.5°. Alternating chills and fever sapped my energy for five miserable days until my doctors eventually concluded that I had Lyme disease.

Physically disoriented and feeling wretched, I was also emotionally pummeled once again. Really? Another roadblock forcing me to come to a stop and reroute my future plans?

My recovery was slow and disheartening. I had always been so active, but now I felt achy and had little energy. With the possibility of returning to school in the fall now definitely not an option, the questions of "What is my purpose?" and "What am I supposed to do now?" began resurfacing.

After two months without purpose, suffering from both an aching body and an aching loneliness, I began to feel restless and wanted to get out of the house—out of Rochester. I thought it would feel good to see family and places I had once lived with Clayton and our family. It was always helpful to be around people who had known him because it helped me feel closer to him. And I just needed to clear my head. It felt like a small but purposeful step in that direction.

I decided that some time with my cousins on Long Island might be a good way to start. Logistically, their home would be a good destination, just an eight-hour drive away, then on to Connecticut for more cousins and to Boston for friends before circling back to Rochester, New York.

When I called, my cousins John and Stef sounded genuinely glad I was going to pay them a visit. Quite naturally Stef asked the question, "Who's coming with you?"

Once again I was hit head-on with the baseball bat of grief. I still managed to say, "It's just me."

I'd been so used to running in a pack—my family—and taking care of everyone else. It hurt to have to say:

*It's just me now.*

The trip was happening, though, and the day I left I was excited and had enough snacks and gear to survive on the road with a family of seven (I hadn't yet learned to scale back). I walked out my door on October 24, 2017, to embark on my first solo road trip in more than thirty-three years.

As I drove alone in the car, I had time to think about the fact that I had always been the one to take care of the needs of those around me.

Was there enough food?

How was I going to divide the labor? *Camilla, you do the packing of the car. Gerrit, you carry everything out to the car.*

I didn't have those responsibilities to occupy me this time. Now I was having to look around me and deeply consider my future and decide what I wanted to do. What did I want to be? What were the values and principles that I wanted to hang on to, and what did I want to let go of in this new life?

While I was having these thoughts, I was overcome with a spiritual as well as physical pain in my heart—a pain still deep and consuming. At least by now I wasn't surprised when I was hit with those pangs of grief. I had learned to breathe in extra air so that when I would breathe out, I could feel as if a weight were literally being lifted.

The pain lessened, but the agonizing thoughts remained. My life had been shattered and ripped away by the accident. Why wasn't *I* taken? Clayton could have done such a wonderful job without me!

He was a wonderful cook. I cooked to survive. In fact, our joke at the dinner table was that he "let" me cook because

I needed the practice.

He handled all the finances. I'd always had a budget for the expenses I handled, but I'd had no hand in the big picture.

He was a garage sale aficionado, a genius at going out on Saturday mornings and finding exactly what I needed. I had no interest in chasing after early-morning bargains. He would've known what to do, while I was just putting one foot in front of the other, doing the best I could and with sometimes messy, hurtful results.

So many questions and no answers. I asked myself as I drove to Long Island, *Is this the way I should keep moving forward?* I could only pray, *Please, God, tell me if I'm going the wrong way.* And I wasn't talking about missing the next highway exit.

Those questions lingered as I visited my cousins and connected with more family, revisiting places Clayton and I had lived together. It was calming to spend time with them and eat and tour together. We talked about interesting things, not just the next task I had to attack.

One day we visited Sagamore Hill National Historic Site. Though it was in the middle of a highly populated area, the home of Theodore Roosevelt was a gorgeous dwelling atop a green hill, an oasis of sorts. As we toured the house, I was struck by the classic design. The signature heads of animals on the walls from Teddy's famous hunting expeditions. The huge library lined with books and rich wood. It was such a manly house and reflected what a unique individual he was.

As I wandered through, I remembered watching a documentary about him and how he had lost the first love of his life, his wife Alice Hathaway Lee. His wife and his mother had died on the same day in 1884, leaving Roosevelt a single father with a two-day-old infant. At the time, I didn't recall this information on an emotional level; my feelings were still somewhat turned off. But I was fascinated by the fact that in his grief, he had left his political career behind and gone west to the Dakota territories, where "the beauty and solitude of the west . . . helped ease the grief of the loss of Alice."[2]

His experience of throwing himself into a new life and new experiences, revitalizing and transforming himself in the process, resonated with me. This experience certainly followed me as I visited Connecticut and Massachusetts, thinking about my past and my future as I walked around Walden Pond. Right then, I just wanted the pain to stop,

---

2 "The Life of Theodore Roosevelt," National Park Service, last modified October 9, 2014, https://www.nps.gov/thri/theodorerooseveltbio.htm.

and yet I couldn't increase the speed at which the healing was happening. My grief had its own timetable. All I knew then was that if I wanted to work through this pain, I had to keep moving forward and press onward.

After I returned home, I spent the winter considering my experience on this road trip. I felt immense pain in my solitude, but I also had some important realizations that came to me as a slow progression of ideas.

I knew I needed to go on a trip. A long trip.

I felt I couldn't just wander aimlessly. I needed a purpose.

It came to me that such a purpose had to arise from my pain, from my loss.

And it slowly dawned on me that what had *caused* that loss was ignorance about tire safety.

Was there something I could do to educate people about something as basic as the tires on their vehicles?

Perhaps I couldn't go back to school and address my weakness in writing, but I could apply strengths I already had to carry this mission out, whatever it actually was. Because of the life Clayton and I had lived, I knew people all across the country, and this network could help me.

My maiden voyage to Long Island, Connecticut, and Massachusetts had also given me the confidence that I could take long trips by myself and the courage to go on even longer adventures. I was confident in my driving skills. I was adventurous. I had an open mind: when an obstacle was in front of me, I could figure out a way around it, over it, or under it. I was determined. I had a great love for others and wanted to help.

Exactly how I could help, I didn't yet know. All I knew was I couldn't change the past but I could make a better future for myself and others. I wanted to find peace through the hope that I might be able to live a new life, transformed because of the love I had shared with Clayton.

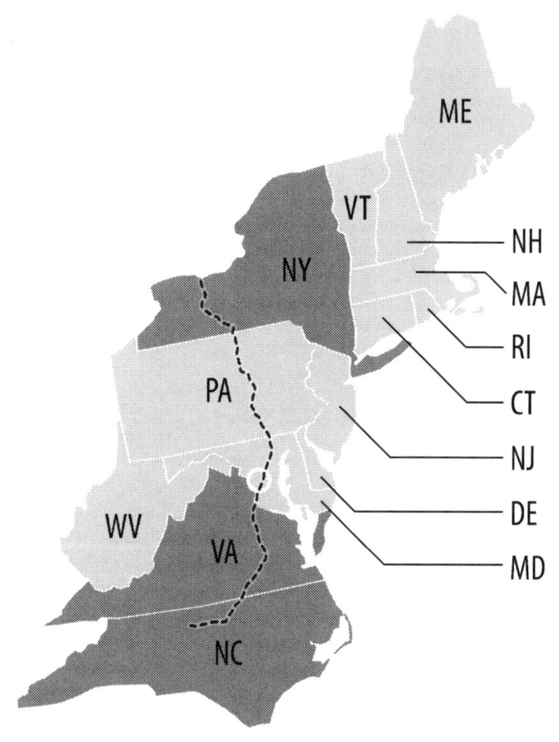


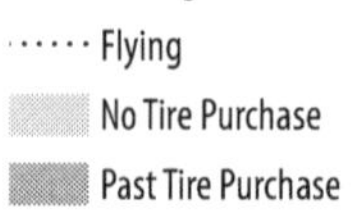


**LOOP 1**

*April 4-12, 2018 (9 days)*

# CHAPTER TWO

## MY UNEXPECTED JOURNEY

| Marcia | Eileen | Annabel |
|---|---|---|
| #1-Virginia | #2-North Carolina | #3-New York |

I can't pinpoint the very moment when that last piece of my plan fell into place. What you need to realize is that I had become wary of plans. I had grandiose plans of downsizing my house in Rochester and moving everything to the West Coast. That didn't work out. I had plans for my retirement with my husband. That didn't work out. I had plans to go back to school. Once again, *that* didn't work out. It made me wonder what was wrong with my planning style.

So now when I make decisions, I imagine the tile floor in my house in Hawaii. Each title was a large square around two feet by two feet. I remember the size because my small dog could curl up on one of these tiles. In my mind, I have a huge tile floor before me of decisions that have to be made to get me to my goal. I take one step onto a big tile—that is, make a decision—and live with that decision and see if I think and feel it's a correct one for me. Sometimes I am able to make many decisions and move along quickly. Other times I stand on a tile for a long time, not knowing what to do or how to do it. So I wait, but I know I will make a decision and I will keep moving.

By the end of that winter, I had already stepped on many tiles and had reached a huge one. I decided to drive to each state—flying to Alaska and Hawaii, of course—learning about the tire safety information provided by all the states and buying someone a new set of tires in each state, all while teaching myself and others about tire safety. At the forefront of my mind was warning people about the dangers of driving on old tires, but at this point, I knew little about tire safety myself and felt that I was as much a student as a teacher.

It felt like the correct decision for me. I knew I was headed in the right direction. Having arrived on that big tile, I actually felt peaceful, calm, and excited at the same time. I had assurance, and by starting my trip, I was putting my faith into action.

For the time being, I kept it to myself.

Obviously I wasn't going to just set out on this ambitious journey without alerting anyone. I tested the waters by first telling my children that I wanted to work on my family history and drive around the lower forty-eight and fly to Alaska and Hawaii. I had a good reason for taking this slow and letting everyone warm up to the idea. We had lost Clayton on a road trip, and I wanted to be considerate of their feelings. I did not hear a voice of concern from any of my four daughters. My son, Gerrit, was out of the country in Japan serving as a missionary for The Church of Jesus Christ of Latter-day Saints, and it seemed better not to tell him about my possible plans, as it might have distracted him from his work.

Just to be clear, I didn't yet tell my children about the true *purpose* of my trip—the education and fact-finding mission. I didn't want them to try to talk me out of it, and I feared that once they knew the details of my plan, they surely would. I already knew it was a risky decision, but I also knew I needed to do it.

I still owned the last car that my husband had bought—a silver 2002 VW Beetle somewhat humorously named Barracuda. I came up with the idea of pulling Barracuda on a trailer behind my Suburban.

Barracuda was a stick shift. Part of our driving plan in our family was that everyone needed to learn how to drive a car with a manual transmission, which is why we'd held on to this car. We also had a fifteen-passenger van (which everyone had to learn to navigate in as well), but I sold it in Hawaii rather than try to ship it to the continental U.S. The VW I could take back to Virginia with me and finish teaching my two youngest the fine art of the stick shift. It was also a way to hold on to some semblance of our family traditions even though Clayton wasn't with us.[1]

My intent was to have tire stores inspect Barracuda's tires and, in applicable states, have inspections done on the entire VW to test the technicians' knowledge and see what information I could gather. I even collected four mismatched tires with different problems to put on Barracuda so that I could ask questions about tires to help me gather data. One of those tires was from the set of tires Barracuda was currently running on, which had only about 5,000 miles, and the tread was fantastic. However, they were from 2012 and were already six years old and getting too old to drive on. At this point in my plan, it was important to me to learn whether tire salespeople understood and believed this principle and would share this information with me.

Naturally, Barracuda, as beloved as it was, wasn't safe to drive through forty-eight states, so at the end of winter, in March, I put my plan into action. I bought myself a trailer. It was made of aluminum—that just so happened to match Barracuda's silver color—and was lightweight for better fuel economy. The trailer was eighteen feet long with two six-foot pull-out ramps that were stored

1 Read Appendix B to learn about another family tradition.

within it. I had to take them out and attach them to the back of the trailer to drive the VW up onto it. Learning all the intricacies that go along with pulling a trailer was complicated, and I felt a great sense of accomplishment having mastered doing this on my own.

Actually, though, I wasn't really alone. I took pictures of each step with my phone as the kind and patient salesman was teaching me. The trailer shop folks positioned the VW and put aluminum blocks on the trailer so I'd know how far to drive the VW up onto it so it would be balanced correctly. In the process, I felt respect and support from all the people involved there. If I had questions, they answered them so I could make the necessary decisions. One tile at a time.

At about 8:30 a.m. on April 4, 2018, I kissed my three dogs goodbye and left them with good friends and drove out of town with Barracuda in tow. The odometer on my Suburban read 120,640 miles and the dash showed a balmy 42°. I was prepared with a full tank of gas and an empty bladder, signs of a true road warrior. This time I'd brought fewer snacks, but I still had an SUV full of stuff.

Although I was traveling by myself, I did not feel alone. My gnome and my Tire Angel were with me. Gimli is a plastic garden gnome that stands about fifteen inches high. He sports a burgundy hat with a brown rucksack over his left shoulder and holds a tall brown walking stick in his right hand, resting it close to his chest. I love his white beard because my father had a beard for most of his life. His shirt is the same color as his hat and is cinched with a black belt, his trousers are forest green, and his feet are shod with black boots to match his black belt.

Gimli rode with me in the front passenger seat of Wolverine—my name for the Suburban. We started together on that very first leg of my journey, with him coming out for photo ops when we came to a new state sign or a place of interest along my travels.

Basically, Gimli reminded me of some lore my immigrant grandfather had told my father: when a young man in Germany came of age, he left his house with a walking stick and a rucksack to seek his fortune. When my own father graduated from high school in 1948, he and a friend left Seymour, Connecticut, and hitchhiked across the United States to California. I felt as if I was following in their footsteps and that Gimli, who also wears a beard and carries a stick and a rucksack, was a good representation of this spirit of adventure in my family.

The Tire Angel was a souvenir from a trip I'd made to Canada in 2012 to find some of my ancestors in the beautiful town of Sainte-Agathe-des-Monts, Quebec. It is a stained glass figurine of an angel that was originally holding a bouquet of pink flowers. I had hung this angel on my rearview mirror, but for this trip I had replaced the flowers with a black plastic pinewood derby wheel as a reminder that I wanted to be a source of safety and goodness in the lives of the people that I would find and buy a set of tires for.

The drive through the green, rolling Pennsylvania mountains was lovely. It was a joy to drive up a hill and reach the summit to see the great expanse of a lush valley before me. Repeating this process with only the effort of putting my foot on the gas pedal was soothing. I hadn't realized the importance of being in nature for my healing at this point in my journey. All I knew was that it felt peaceful to be on the road again.

Wolverine handled the trailer well, and Washington, DC, traffic was better than expected, so I arrived at my first daughter Celesta's home in time for dinner. I knew she was a wise choice for my first stop. Always able to handle changes with remarkable ease, Celesta looks at life as an adventure. Her positive outlook and awareness of her strengths and weaknesses help her to be a good problem solver, and I am continually amazed at how she consistently takes action towards her meaningful goals. Is it any wonder I thought she'd understand my plan quite well?

But when I pulled up to her apartment to find her waiting outside for me, her beautiful red hair like a familiar beacon, her astonished expression and wide eyes told me that my daughter, always so in control of her emotions, was in complete shock.

As soon as I got out of the Suburban, I read *Mom, what are you DOING?* all over her face. I thought now I would be able to share the big picture of what I would be doing on my trip. But I was also saddened by her apparent concern, and that impression made me exercise some consideration for *her* feelings. So at the moment, I didn't say a word.

Instead, we left immediately to go out for dinner. My daughter is a foodie and knows all the good restaurants, and her choice that night did not disappoint. Over delicious hot and spicy individual-sized pizza, we talked about, of course, food, what was going on in her life, and my plans for my trip.

She was quiet on the way back to her home and during our climb to her second-story apartment. But as soon as we walked inside, she motioned to her dining room table and said, "Mom, let's sit down and talk."

She was serious and calm, her voice steady and measured. In fact, I even got out paper and pencil, because I knew it was going to be that kind of conversation, and because I respected her and wanted to hear what she had to say.

There was no beating around the bush. Celesta led with, "Mom, you can't do this."

"And why can't I do this?" I said.

With love and distress in her voice, she shared with me her concerns about the trip. I listened patiently, though inside my mind I was thinking, *I am a grown woman and your mother! I can do what I need to do.*

She had her reasons, and I had answers:

> Celesta: There have been some really bad trailer accidents because trailers weren't balanced correctly.
>
> Me: The trailer shop made sure it was balanced.
>
> Celesta: It's hard driving a trailer.
>
> Me: I've been practicing. I can even back the trailer up into the driveway now.
>
> Celesta: What about—
>
> Me: I have the brake system from the Suburban connected to the trailer. I know how to secure the straps. I really have done everything right.

"But why do it at all?" was her next query. Couldn't I educate people about tire safety using social media? Pencil in hand, I listened to her talk about blogging and Facebook and Twitter—things so not in my world. It would take some time to create a following, she said, but I could . . .

As she continued to talk, I became more discouraged. I didn't know that world, and I wasn't ready to learn about it at that time. I needed to go on this trip, and nothing was going to deter me. Yet I knew Celesta loved me, and her concerns were all for my well-being. She'd already lost one parent on the road and, even as strong as she was, I didn't want her to lose another one.

So I sat back and let her give me the rest of her reasons for so very intently trying to talk me out of this. The very first one grabbed me.

"Mom, you are too kind and trusting to pull off something like this! People might take advantage of you."

She might have me there, so I nodded her on.

"You need to build on your strengths," she said.

That was a pivotal moment. I felt so broken inside, and yet she saw strength in me? Strength other people had failed to see? Some had made it clear that I had limited skills in their eyes, and all the years I had spent taking care of other people didn't equate to marketable expertise that translated to the workplace. After all, I'd been a stay-at-home mom for thirty-three years. Celesta's apprehension about my plan stung because it hit on insecurities I was already feeling. I was so driven to accomplish my goal, but was I truly too limited to make it happen? Even I had only recently rediscovered some of the strengths that had given me the confidence to start this journey.

I thanked my daughter for sharing her thoughts and concerns and lay in bed pondering what she'd said.

I have a nightly routine: I pray, write in my journal, read scriptures, and then read a fantasy book to relax and fall asleep. That night, I dwelled mostly on the prayer portion of that routine, asking—mightily—for help and understanding. I had felt that I was supposed to go on this trip—but was now the right time? And if so, how was I going to make this work?

Celesta's words about playing to my strengths kept coming back to me. One of the fundamental strengths that would carry me forward was how I *cared* about people being safe. This strength had been developed by the extensive practice I'd had *caring* for other people. Yes, I *had* been a stay-at-home mom for over thirty-three years, and that *meant* something. I thought of my Tire Angel figurine. Just like angels, a mom does the sometimes invisible and thankless work of loving, caring for, and safeguarding her children and others she loves. Now I wanted to become that "angel"—that mom—in other people's lives with regard to tires.

I would become The Tire Mom.

This title captured the sense of responsibility I felt with my mission. It wasn't about the gimmick with Barracuda. It was about the urgent need to share what I believed was life-saving information. Though it was difficult to put myself out there, this identity would give my mission a unified public persona that communicated the love and protection I wanted to spread. I felt grateful that my talk with Celesta led to this important step in truly clarifying what the trip ahead of me was really about.

When I left Celesta's home, little did I realize the concern and worry I'd triggered in all of my children. Over the next few days, I heard from each of them. Driving and talking on speaker phone, I heard their cases against my trip, trailer or no trailer.

Two of my daughters had seen horrific traffic accidents in the western United States involving cars and trailers.

One of my daughters was already having nightmares in which she couldn't find me.

The other was more worried about who would be responsible for organizing my affairs if I died.

Between that and pointing out that I had so little experience navigating a trailer in traffic and voicing opinions about fuel economy, they were putting a full court press on me.

And their fears weren't just about the driving. My idea of camping solo also caused them to be extremely uneasy. They had seen too many crime shows.

Clearly I was causing them deep anxiety, and I couldn't just ignore that. It's true what American businessman and religious leader M. Russell Ballard once wisely said: "There is no problem in the family . . . that cannot be solved if we look for solutions in the Lord's way by counseling—really counseling—with each other."[2]

We took turns talking through the issues and hearing each other's perspectives. We presented different ideas in an effort to come up with solutions we could all live with. I felt that I needed to go on this trip. That was not negotiable, and I said they needed to respect that. In terms of *how* I was going to do it, I was willing to be flexible and considerate of their feelings and take their concerns into account.

It was decided that after I went to my first two states I would sell the trailer and Barracuda and put the mismatched tires in the back of my Suburban, so that I could ask questions and have a consistent physical learning tool about tires along the way. It would be easier to drive without the trailer, and it would also be safer and more economical. I also promised to text my children every night and let them know that I was safe and behind a door for the evening—at a friend's house or at a hotel. As it turned out, one of my daughters, unbeknownst to

---

2 Russell M. Ballard, *Counseling with Our Councils: Learning to Minister Together in the Church and in the Family* (Salt Lake City: Deseret Book, 2012), loc. 144, Kindle.

me, had my phone tracked so that she could always see where I was.

I learned something incredibly valuable from that experience. We often confine others (and ourselves) to neat, little boxes. We have ideas about what they can do and cannot do. When they act out of that box, it can be stressful for all involved.

As a mother, I have always wanted my children to try new and different things in life. I want them to be happy and fulfilled in their endeavors. With Clayton gone and having just become an empty nester, *I* could now do new and different things. It was hard for them to see me take risks and be out on my own, even if it was what I needed in order to become the person I knew I could become.

Of course it is important that those acting out of the confines of their boxes make good choices. But ultimately, the responsibility always rests with the individual making the choice. This was a good experience for my family to learn about labels, boundaries, and how to support each other in a loving way.

Now I was willing to take the risk and keep moving forward—to that next tile in front of me.

After my fruitful visit with Celesta, it was time to get back on the road and visit my first state, Virginia, in my official capacity as The Tire Mom. The first set of tires I would purchase would be for my friend Marcia. Marcia and I had become close when we lived in Williamsburg while my husband Clayton taught MBA students at the College of William & Mary. Her tires were old and worn, and it felt good to be able to help. After buying the tires, we spent some time driving along the Colonial Parkway eating sweets from the Wythe Candy & Gourmet Shop and sipping root beer. As we drove by the Yorktown Pier, memories flashed through my mind and heart of Clayton teaching the girls how to fish and catch crabs off the end of the pier. After this painful yet sweet memory, I looked down the pier again, thinking that this was the beginning of my journey and wondering where it would take me and if I was really going to be able to heal from the hurt and the loss of losing Clayton.

As I drove south down Route 85 to my next state, North Carolina, I evaluated what went well with the purchase of the tires for Marcia and what could have gone better. I believe in taking small purposeful steps when I am doing something new and different. At this point, I didn't really have a strategy, and now was the time to make mistakes so that I could learn from them and be ready for the next forty-nine purchases. For one thing, my resolve to ditch the trailer when I returned to Rochester was solidified, as I was already noticing that the trailer was a distraction. People were focusing on the trailer rather than the tires. Moreover, the whole concept with Barracuda was becoming a distraction for me as well. I realized I would need to implement some changes for the next state. For this first Tire Mom purchase, I had let Marcia choose where to buy tires and what tires to buy. During the experience, I had mostly focused on trying to test the tire salesman's knowledge of tire safety issues using the old tires on Barracuda. Though I had felt relief in getting my friend new tires, my focus should have been on verifying she understood why she should continue to check her tires in the future.

In North Carolina I purchased tires for my friend Eileen, and while I accomplished my main objective, I was still fine-tuning my strategy. Eileen and I had been friends since our children had spent a year together in high school, and it was comforting to be with her and her family. She had picked out the best auto shop in town to replace her tires. Though I didn't spend much time discussing whether she had problems with her tires, I remember having an overwhelming feeling of calm knowing that I was teaching my friends how to read the sides of their tires so they could teach others and make the roads a safer place. All tires have an abundance of information printed on the sidewall but you must know how to find and interpret it. Tires have the letters DOT printed on them, followed by a series of numbers and letters indicating the manufacturing facility code, the tire size code, the manufacturer identity number, and finally, four numbers officially called the tire identification number (but what I affectionately named the "Tire Halo") that indicate the week and year the tire was made. For instance a Tire Halo containing "2519" means that the tire was made in the twenty-fifth week of 2019. After explaining this to Eileen, I learned to minimize the distracting information and instead concentrated on sharing the key information about the DOT as the focus of my mission.

I finished my first loop by returning to New York, which was the third state on my journey. This purchase was related to a few decisions that I followed through on once I was home. I followed through on my commitment to sell Barracuda and the trailer. Since the car was the last car my husband had owned, I wanted it to go to a good family. My friend Deborah knew that her daughter Annabel had always wanted a VW Bug so I sold Barracuda to her.

Before I sold the car, I headed to my local tire store to take the mismatched tires off of Barracuda and get new tires for Annabel. The workers at my tire store know that I am very vigilant about my tires. I asked them to set aside the mismatched tires from the VW because I wanted to keep them for the research component of my summer road trip. I then requested to have brand-new 2018 tires put on the VW. Because tire age is a significant factor in tire safety, you want new tires that you buy to be as fresh off the manufacturing line as possible. Even if they have never been driven on and have deep tread, tires still have a finite lifespan. The tire store employees agreed to give me a set of 2018 (the current year) tires, and I went home while they installed them. When I returned to pick the car up, I simply checked to make sure they had put the old tires in the back of the VW and drove home, trusting that they had fulfilled my request for 2018 tires.

The next day, however, I checked and realized that the Tire Halo on Barracuda's new tires did not contain the digits I expected: they were from 2017. I went back to the store more than a little upset. I had trusted them and they did not deliver as promised. I spoke with the same salesman and told him that he did not fulfill what he had said he would do. He put his hands in the air and said, "You drove off the lot."

I was dumbstruck. Then I thought, "You don't know who you're dealing with! I am The Tire Mom and I am going to put this story in my book!" I learned that day that I couldn't take what the tire technician says at face value, I had to verify for myself what the Tire Halo said on every set of tires I purchased before driving away off the lot.

Annabel became my third Tire Mom purchase, since she bought my car with the "new" 2017 tires on them after I explained the situation to her and Deborah. Over the next few months, I was to learn that issues like the one I experienced were far too common.

I had made some valuable progress on Loop 1. Though I was still struggling emotionally with wondering if I could ever heal, I had witnessed that taking small steps can still lead to great progress. Abandoning the trailer and selling Barracuda had simplified and focused my project, showing me the value of collaborating with people, which had been a struggle for me as I sought to overcome the labels that were put on me after my husband's death, and of trusting in and standing up for myself. I felt ready to take on Loop 2, but I would soon learn that I hadn't worked out all the kinks in my plan.

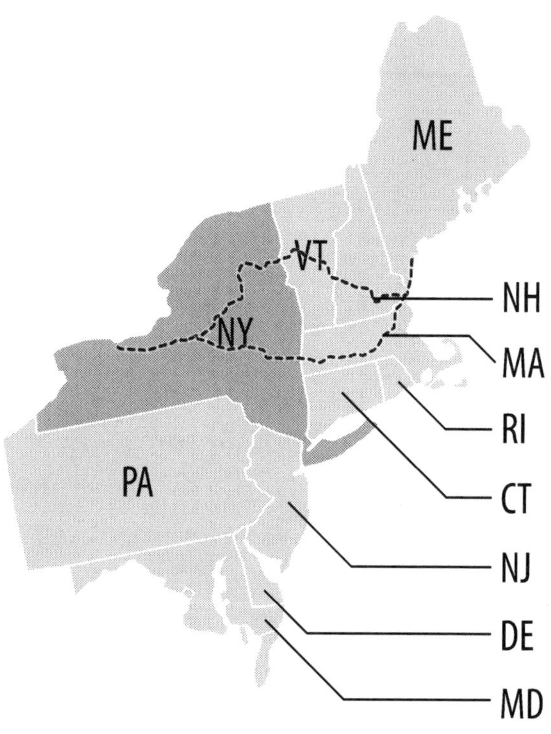


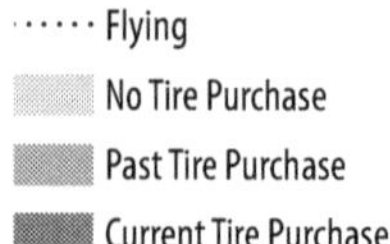


**LOOP 2**

*May 4-9, 2018 (6 days)*

# CHAPTER THREE

## DOING IT MY WAY

Loop 2 started out wonderfully on Friday, May 4, 2018. I had spent the winter thinking I was going to make my journey with Barracuda and a trailer in tow. Now that my daughters had convinced me that it was not the best idea, I had to admit that I felt lighter, not just because I was no longer pulling what felt like a ton behind me (both literally and figuratively) but also because I knew the decision to make the trek in Wolverine without a trailer was a good one. Between the increased gas mileage I would obtain without a trailer and the reduced risk without Barracuda in tow, I was ready on every level to go out and try this thing again.

This second loop would encompass Maine, Massachusetts, Rhode Island, and Connecticut. As I pulled out of the driveway, though, I knew I was taking a baby step toward a bigger plan. I was only setting my sights on four states, all of them relatively close to home, because I wanted to take this one small step at a time. I also wanted to get these northeastern states done at a time when I wouldn't have to drive through the blizzard-like conditions that the northeast is known for in winter.

Gimli, my Tire Angel, and I made our six-hour way through the Adirondack Mountains toward picturesque

Heart Lake, which I try to visit at least once a year and where I was to stay in the lodge. This weekend was to be a trip for pleasure—revisiting the familiar, but on my own terms. Along the way, I relived the memories of our family adventures in this neck of the woods: hiking up Mount Marcy and Mount Jo, the seven of us sleeping in tents, making s'mores over campfires. Clayton and I were being frugal. The kids thought we were on five-star vacations—and we were, in our own unique way. Clayton's stories were always what made those evenings around the many campfires stand out all these years later.

My husband was a master storyteller. He had the uncanny ability to captivate all of us—from the littlest toddler all the way up to me—with his hilarious stories of hijinks and mischief. His facial expressions brought the story to life, and it was as if we were standing right there with him as the story unfolded around us. His tone moved smoothly up and down to match the pace of the plot, and his pauses said as much as his words.

The children, of course, giggled and chimed in on the ones they'd heard over and over. When a yarn was completely spun, they begged for him to tell another story, which, of course, he did.

Recalling those magical times could have caused me emotional pain that day, but I felt driven to move forward. Just then I wasn't ready to deal with the pain. Besides, this experience would be different for me. I'd never stayed in the lodge before or even eaten there. When you have a party of seven, it gets more than a little expensive—and most places understandably frown on you piling three or four people into one bed.

As I drove up the two-lane road toward the lodge, a mist formed across my path. I could feel the tension of a storm in the air, the kind that makes the hairs on your arms stand up. Just as I pulled into the parking lot and turned off the engine, the clouds seemed to explode, and a deluge of rain pounded the Suburban. I had never *seen* such a downpour. It struck me that if I had dawdled at all en route rather than pushing on, I would be driving in this, and that clearly would have been dangerous.

The wind blew the rain almost sideways as I ran into the lodge to check in. Even just being out in that quick moment I felt—and probably looked—like a wet hunting dog, soaking hair sticking to my head, my clothes clinging to my body like a second skin.

After putting myself together a little, I went to the dining room and sat down on a bench at the long white pine table. My first order of business was to look at the storm raging outside the window and be thankful that I didn't have to try to set up a tent or start a fire.

Later that night when I snuggled into that warm, dry bed—just before the power went out—and listened to the gusts rattling the trees (gusts I later learned reached sixty miles per hour), I thanked God for being dry. In addition to all my outdoor experiences with my husband and our clan, I grew up in Colorado, where my family of origin camped regularly in what we called "tube tents" that all but collapsed in less volatile storms than this. Yes. I was VERY grateful to be in a comfortable, dry bed indoors.

As the weekend unfolded, I began to settle in with the other guests at the lodge, all of whom had stories to tell, and as we got to know each other they encouraged me to tell some of my own stories. They were intrigued as I related my recent exploits on the educational mission I was conducting. On Sunday, I went to a tiny nearby church—something else I'd never done when visiting Lake Placid before—and overheard folks talking about how they'd helped each other after the power outage, hoisting chain saws and sharing food. I wasn't part of that community, but it brought me great comfort to see people banding together in times of trouble.

During my stay at the lodge, there was one special conversation with another guest that really hit home for me. I was sitting across the pine table from a short, light-haired man with shoulders like an iron worker, who had a look about him that could only be described as solid. Through the course of the meal he began to describe his journey.

"Right now I'm trying to get back on the trail," he said.

"Back on it?" I asked. To me, he looked like he'd never left it.

He nodded ruefully. "My son and I started hiking the Appalachian Trail several years ago—a stretch at a time. He lost interest but I kept doing different sections.

"Last year, I was getting near the end of the trail, up in Maine, and I tore my ACL, but we're still going to finish." The hiker went on: "But I have to get back into it. And hiking is the only way to do that."

By now I was leaning into the table—and probably dipping my hair into my baked beans. I said, "I love hiking and backpacking, but I want to do more. What advice would you give me?"

He gave me a square, straight-on, steady look. Then he said, "You do it *your* way."

While everyone else at the table nodded and grunted agreement and launched into their own hiking experiences, I felt myself slump right there on the pine bench. Do it *my way?* He might as well have been speaking a foreign language.

At this point in my journey, I didn't know how to do that, at least not consciously. But something in me comprehended this advice on a subconscious level, and such things can take time to truly become conscious. I didn't realize at the time that if I was to move forward, I was going to have to leave many unnecessary, heavy things behind one piece at a time, just as I had done with Barracuda and the trailer. My way, tile by tile, was to continually lighten the load so I could find greater freedom, liberation, and empowerment.

The people I interacted with weren't the only part of that Adirondack weekend that stayed with me. Nature itself teaches me, which I relate to God because God, among other things, *is* nature. As I spent time alone out there, I had the image of a cup in my mind. A shattered ceramic cup that needed to be pieced back together. Obviously I couldn't reattach those pieces back into the perfect cup it was before, and that wasn't going to happen with my shattered self either. But I could feel myself coming together again as I soaked in nature's beauty and did things I'd never done before. I wasn't going to be the same woman I was before Clayton's accident. I was taking a new shape, and the river of life I was in was going to determine that shape.

On Monday, I set out for Maine—Kenebunkport to be exact. Wolverine, Gimli, my Tire Angel, and I took a small ferry across Lake Champlain. Those thirty minutes felt like an adventure to me as I discovered that the lake comes down from Canada and separates New York from Vermont. Because the banks are not populated and the terrain is rural, I could imagine I was back in the 1800s as a pioneer woman. Metaphorically I was, as I pushed outward on my own uncharted frontier. As this new pioneer persona sunk in, I took in the little white churches with their pointed steeples, the rustic fences, and the broken-down barns with their grayed wood.

Once I was on land again, though, I got back into race-to-the-finish mode. I only made two stops along the way for bathroom breaks because I wanted to get to the DMV in Kennebunkport. With my comfortably familiar Harry Potter audiobooks playing, I mulled over this part of my journey. I wanted to understand what the newest drivers learn as they study the driver manual provided for them by the DMV to ideally become safe operators of their vehicles. To get the context of what was taught, I planned to collect one such manual from each state along the way—hence my focus on getting to the DMV in Kennebunkport before it closed.[1]

I was rather proud of myself for arriving at the DMV at 4:30 p.m., well before the doors locked. That feeling lasted about seven seconds because as I reached for the small wallet I kept clipped to the front pocket of my jeans, I discovered it was no longer there.

I didn't panic immediately; it had to be in the car somewhere. It held my license, my credit card, my health insurance, my car insurance . . . everything I needed to have for this road trip. It didn't take long for the search to become frantic.

The only thing to do was call my friends Holly and Mike and let them know I'd be late because I had to backtrack to the two rest stops I'd pulled into. That meant driving ninety minutes one way. My audiobook now on mute, I prayed the entire time, prayers that all sounded like, *I've got to find this! I've got to do this!* What if somebody was at that moment using my card?

What if I was stopped by a state trooper, and I didn't have my driver's license? What if I got in an

---

*1* If you'd like to learn more about this, you can start by checking out the graph in Appendix F. Visit your local DMV office or state website for further information.

accident and nobody could identify me? As I reached first one rest stop and then the other, I went through a thorough routine. I retraced my steps. I scoured the bathrooms and stalls (with my eyes, that is) but to no avail. My last hope was to find the information desk and beg the attendant to tell me some good news about my missing wallet. "Discouraged" falls far short of how I felt as I climbed back into the Suburban and drove my dejected self back to Kennebunkport. At that point, I'd spent four hours looking for my lost wallet with nothing to show for it.

It was 8:30 p.m. when I pulled into the driveway of my friends' place. We had met when Holly had been attending the University of Rochester School of Medicine and Dentistry to become an ER doctor. I used to go to her husband's cooking classes. They were kind and understanding of my situation, and I was finally able to get some rest. I woke up the next morning saddened that I would not be able to continue this second loop and had to go home with no license and no money.

I needn't have worried. My generous friends presented me with enough money to buy a tank of gas and have lunch on the way back to Rochester. I was beyond grateful, but accepted the money as a loan, which I paid back as soon as I got home. Not only was I not helping people, but now people were bailing me out.

I then had to contact all the people I'd arranged to meet and buy tires for on this loop. Were they understanding? Of course. Did they express sadness for me? Without a doubt. But all I could think about was what else was surely going through their heads: *Here's this woman who we already think is nuts for driving all over creation putting tires on strangers' cars. Now she's gone and lost all her essential belongings. How on Earth is she going to do this?* And how could I even answer back to these imaginary statements when it was exactly what I was feeling about myself too?

I made my way home, thinking over the whole ordeal for seven hours. My head was not in the game. I couldn't be leaving my stuff everywhere. Everything now depended on my awareness. I had to make decisions and accept the consequences of those decisions.

As I drove and wrestled with this, a conversation came to mind that I had with my father many years earlier. I was in college and had come home for a few months, so we were working on his boat together in the garage. Seemingly out of the blue, he said, "Diana, you're being a pigeon."

"A *what?*" I replied.

"A pigeon. You're leaving your droppings all over the house. Clean it up!"

I wished I could have argued with him, but I couldn't. Because when I went into the house, I saw that indeed I *had* left my droppings—or rather, my stuff—all over the place. I quickly gathered up my belongings and deposited them in my room.

Yet here I was, guilty of pigeon behavior once again, droppings left everywhere. I needed to hold onto my stuff and keep it all in one place.

This part of my journey was not fun, and before I reached Rochester, I had come to an important conclusion: I wanted to be a problem-solver, not a woman who dwells on mistakes. This was a life lesson: learn from your mistakes and then move on with the lesson learned so mistakes are not repeated.

The solution to this problem—besides getting a new license, new credit cards, and jeans with front pockets large enough to safely stow my wallet (curse those jeans with the shallow front pockets just small enough to serve no purpose or function!)—was a back-up plan. If I lost anything when I was on the Western loop, I wouldn't be able to just run home and get another set of keys or a new wallet. And not only that, as I traveled to the fifty states,

I would be spending the night in different locations, including other people's homes. I had to keep track of my stuff. I couldn't afford to leave my droppings.

Before I left home again, I purchased a money belt to wear under my clothes. I had an extra set of keys for Wolverine and some extra cash, along with my passport, a new credit card, and a new health insurance card.

It wasn't just the practical things I attended to, though. Preparing for my next loop with that recent experience so fresh in my mind, I also considered the larger loss in my life yet again. That obviously saddened me, so I decided to seek out some comfort by watching a DVD of Clayton giving a devotional address at BYU-Hawaii on October 11, 2011. My dear husband was an inspired speaker and, as I've mentioned before, a great storyteller. Hearing his voice and seeing his face was reassuring. It was as though he spoke to me and said, "Here, Diana. Watch the devotional." The talk was on loss. After presenting the point that not all epic journeys and adventures have happy endings, he went on to say,

> *The travelers (of old) were left to their own devices or the wisdom of their traveling companions when it came to coping with unexpected perils encountered along the way.*

*To have any chance of returning home, it was important that the traveler not give up hope, no matter how difficult the challenges that they faced.*[2]

Clayton couldn't have known how perfectly this would describe how I now felt traveling the road of life without him. I had been left to my own devices, and I had encountered unexpected perils. I had lost my husband and my purpose in life. I was an empty nester. I felt broken inside. Where was I supposed to go and what was I supposed to do? Should I develop my skills and find a place in the workforce? What had lasting value to me and those around me? But despite these questions and the setbacks I recently experienced, I still had hope, however faint it might be. What, then, did it look like for me to take on the charge that Clayton left at the end of his inspired devotional: "Forget yourself and live a life worth losing."

---

2 To read the text of Clayton's devotional, see Appendix B, or Clayton Hubner, "To Live a Life Worth Losing" (devotional, Laie, Hawaii, October 4, 2011), BYU-Hawaii Speeches, https://devotional.byuh.edu/index.php/node/1726. To view a video recording of the talk online, see Clayton Hubner, "Dr. Clayton Hubner," YouTube video, 40:26, posted by BYU-Hawaii Learning Channel, https://www.youtube.com/watch?v=o6waoTFNM44.

I thought of a book that Richie Norton, one of Clayton's students, had written: *The Power of Starting Something Stupid*. In the book, Norton poses the following question:

> *What is your personal why? Defining the reasons you're working toward your high aspirations is the first and greatest way to work toward overcoming debilitating fears. You may be able to squeak by for a short time on will alone, but when the going gets tough . . . and fear begins to rear its ugly head, you're in for a rude awakening if you don't have an equally powerful why to which you're solidly connected. People successfully overcome fear when the "why" behind what they're afraid of is bigger than the fear itself.*[3]

I had fear, but I knew my primary "why:" I wanted the pain to stop. I somehow sensed that the only way to make that happen was to continue on this trip, get back out there on the road, and try again. As my daughters had

---

3 Richie Norton, *The Power of Starting Something Stupid: How to Crush Fear, Make Dreams Happen, and Live Without Regret*. (Salt Lake City: Shadow Mountain, 2013), 125-126.

pointed out, I could build my plan around my strengths and put up safety nets around my weaknesses.

And I had to do this without trying to hold onto what I used to have while those broken pieces of myself were taken down the river. I would emerge on the surface with my great love for my family, friends . . . for everyone. I could protect them and teach them about this one thing, the Tire Halo, so that they wouldn't have to suffer as I had.

Each time I helped someone, another piece of myself, my real self, would find its way back to me. Person by person, my broken heart would be put back together again.

Next step then. Next tile. I sat down and planned Loop 3.

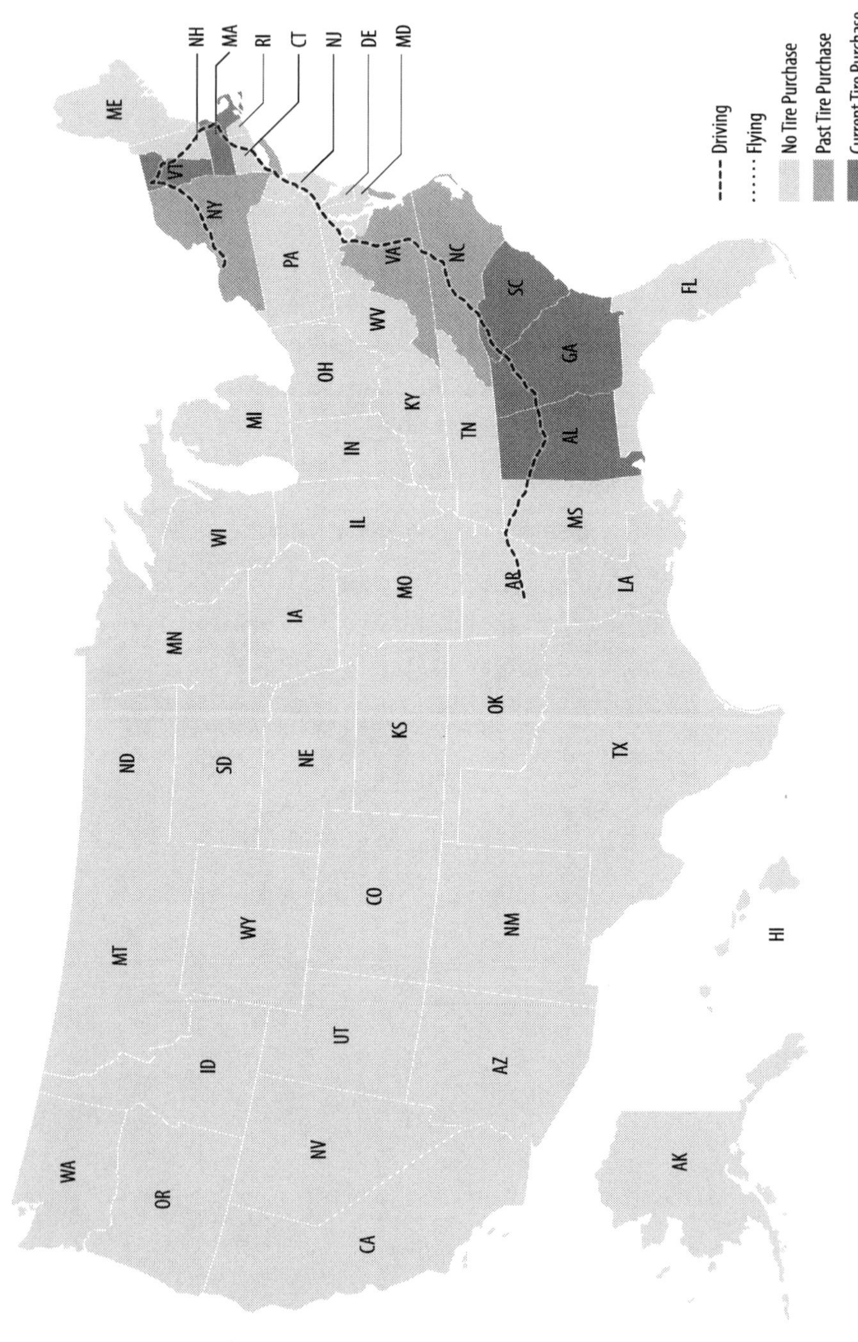


**LOOP 3**

*May 30 - June 15, 2018 (17 days)*

# CHAPTER FOUR

## DIVINE ENCOUNTERS

I left Rochester on May 30, 2018, after yet another delay. My dog Jack had injured his leg. As the saying goes, life is what happens while we're making other plans. At least I was learning to be more flexible, even if the circumstances weren't ideal.

Improvise. Adapt. Overcome.

I felt like I really had to overcome on Loop 3. It was important for me to be back home from Vermont, Massachusetts, South Carolina, Georgia, Alabama, Arkansas, Tennessee, and Kentucky by June 17, 2018. That marked six years to the day since Clayton's accident, and the children and I agreed that I should not be driving on that day.

I gave myself additional incentive by signing up for a writing workshop in Rochester on June 16. The idea for this book was already taking shape, and I wanted to get a better understanding of what was involved in writing and publishing. Doing things I'd never done before was becoming more natural to me.

So once again, I drove through the Adirondacks, following quaint two-lane roads to that bridge that would take me across Lake Champlain one more time. It felt satisfying to be back on the road. I was in go mode, and it was all about getting the job done and putting my feelings to the side. I was surprised how alive I felt. So much of me had changed in these six years.

The sunset was stunning as I crossed the lake toward Colchester, Vermont. I haven't mentioned what sunsets are for me. When I was growing up in Colorado, our backyard faced west so that we could see Mount Evans. In the summer, my parents ended the day by sitting outside watching the sun sink down behind the mountain, leaving it a silhouette before an orange and purple sky. They seemed to have some of their best talks there, and although the thought of those marital conversations made me long for Clayton, I also found comfort in the familiarity of seeing the sun make its slow departure for the night. Life, it seemed, would always be a mixture of longing and comfort.

I didn't linger on those thoughts, because Tire Mom recipient #4 was on my mind. My New York friends, Jamie and her husband, had lived in Vermont when he was in medical school, so I'd asked her if she knew anyone who might need a set of tires there. She'd helped me make contact with a woman named Kayla. So far, I only knew her through texting. I'd told her, as I always do, that I would be the tall redhead.

Kayla and I finally met face-to-face for the first time in the tire store. Kayla was a slender young woman with a kind and giving nature and a little family—a husband who was then in medical school and an adorable infant son, whom they passed back and forth during our time together. It was actually, to my surprise, the tire salesman who put us all at ease.

His question, "What kind of tires are you looking for?" was met with blank stares. I had so much to learn, and I was about to digest a banquet of information.

The tire technician, now taking on a teaching role, pointed out the tire halo to us and explained to Kayla and her husband what the different parts of it meant.

Our next step was to look at Kayla's tires, which were perfect candidates for a Tire Mom replacement. Two of the tires had a great deal of wear. One was as bald as Patrick Stewart. Another had a date of 14/08 in the Tire Halo, making it four years past the recommended replacement date. This little group was about to make some family visits out on the road, and I was glad they would be doing their visits on a safe new set of tires.

It was real now. I was possibly saving the lives of this precious family. And what made it more real was holding the baby boy while his parents signed the paperwork. He had a lot more living to do, and I was playing a role in hopefully ensuring that this would happen.

While the tires were being put on, Kayla and her husband took me out for breakfast. I can think of few better ways to get to know people than over pancakes. The discovery that they were living on a graduate school budget only made the happiness I felt at being able to help them even sweeter. I remembered those financially tight days when Clayton was working on his PhD. It was far too easy to put off purchases like new tires in the interest of keeping food on the table and the lights on.

With Kayla, her husband, and their baby safely on their way, I treated myself to the treasures Vermont offers: the Vermont Teddy Bear Factory (the hotel where I stayed had a huge bear on the bed, the perfect photo op for Gimli and me) and the factory where Ben and Jerry's ice cream is made. My timing was perfect; I arrived just as a tour was starting. Along my journey I made sure to appreciate the joys that each state had to offer, and devouring some Ben & Jerry's ice cream certainly brought me joy that day.

My next stop on my journey wasn't for the purpose of finding someone to give tires to. I just wanted to see

David, a close friend and roommate of Clayton's from the college days. As I've said, seeing and talking with people who knew my husband helped me feel closer to him. David, a middle school Spanish teacher, is a great guy, as one would expect of anyone who has devoted their career to educating middle school adolescents. David has a love of family history, which is one of my hobbies as well. In our time together, he was kind enough to help me find some of my extended family members in old census records. It was so fun hearing his memories of Clayton as we did so, and the time just flew by.

Eventually the conversation turned to my current passion project. By this point on my trip, if anyone showed even the slightest interest in what I was doing, I was ready to share as much information as they were willing to receive. It wasn't long before we were headed out to his car and kneeling on the ground to check out his tires. We found 2017 in all his Tire Halos.

"I'm frugal," David told me. "But I always spend good money on tires."

I found myself wishing everyone could say that.

As I headed for Massachusetts, I realized that these unexpected opportunities to educate and *be* educated were becoming some of my favorite parts of the tire journey. I was learning to be open to those opportunities and to not be afraid to go on detours, which was turning out to be essential to discovering and developing new parts of myself. Clayton knew so much about so many things and was a natural teacher and storyteller, so I often deferred to him. He could tell the tale or teach the concept so much better, and I liked to watch him in his element. Now I was turning into a teacher. I had a potentially lifesaving information to share.

On the morning of June 2, I met my friend Jenn just outside of Boston. Previously, Jenn had lived in Syracuse, New York, and we had worked together as camp directors at a girls' summer camp. Her family had since moved when her husband got a job near Boston, and I didn't get to see her nearly as much as I would have liked. However, like with any strong friendship, we were able to pick up right where we had left off.

After we spent some time catching up, I asked her if she knew anyone who was in need of a set of new tires. She said she thought her friend Linnea needed new tires, so she got her on the phone and presented her with my offer.

Linnea couldn't believe what she was hearing.

Who could blame her? It's very unusual for someone to arrive in town, virtually out of the blue, and offer to buy a set of tires for you. Someone who doesn't even know you. Tires are one of the most expensive purchases necessary for car maintenance, so when Linnea was baffled by the offer, it was understandable.

Linnea even said, "This kind of thing just doesn't happen to me. I don't win the lottery."

Finally, I asked Jenn to turn the phone over to me. I'm not sure whether it was my passion, my straightforward manner, or the agreement I proposed, but she relented to meeting us at the tire store.

The deal I made was that I would buy her two tires, and we'd have the tire technician check the others.

After meeting such resistance, I was relieved when the tire technician at the store pointed out that all the tires on her vehicle needed to be replaced. It was clear he wasn't just trying to make a sale. Two were visibly worn and all four had old dates in their Tire Halos.

This man really knew what he was talking about. He taught me a valuable lesson that day as well. He explained the importance of writing out the information on your Tire Halo and having it easily accessible in your vehicle. I personally use a worksheet that I've included in Appendix G for you to cut out or photocopy. To some this may not be the best way to record this information, but having some way of tracking the various details about your tires is very important.

Linnea had been so skeptical that morning, I was relieved when she showed up at the tire store. After the tires were purchased, she showed overwhelming gratitude for the gift she had received. Her family had fallen on one of those seasons of hard times we all experience now and then. That day, she could go home and tell her kids something good, that someone helped them and that someone had been kind to them. I find it discouraging that such a small act of kindness has become so uncommon that it could be considered such a momentous occasion.

As for me, I had the realization that not everyone trusts generosity. Many have come to believe through bad experiences that when someone offers you a free gift there must be strings attached. However, for my gifts there were no strings attached. The reward for me was in thwarting potential accidents and saving lives. On top of that I was enjoying a beautiful journey in the process. For the rest of my stay in Boston, I felt glimmers of joy seeping into my heart. I relived such wonderful memories of my family including visiting the Public Garden, swimming in Walden Pond in Concord, and going to the Boston LDS Temple. Those memories were becoming far less painful, and far more sweet.

As I made the fifteen-and-a-half-hour drive to South Carolina with a one-night respite spent with my daughter Celesta (who was quite happy to see me without a trailer in tow), I began to look forward to the Southern hospitality I was about to experience. Having lived in Williamsburg, Virginia, for five years, I knew how friendly and welcoming the people could be.

Once Clayton and I had made friends with people, we did our best to keep them in our lives no matter how many miles separate us. When I needed a tire recipient for South Carolina, I thought of my friend Marcia who used to live there. Marcia and I have known each other for over thirty-five years, having both served missions for our church in California in the early 1980s. She knew Patty from her time in South Carolina, and though Marcia now lived in Utah, we all connected by phone. Patty led me to my next Tire Mom candidate, her son fittingly named Clayton.

I met up with Patty at a restaurant. Through our conversation, I learned that she was not only raising several children but also was going back to school and learning about computers, and had recently started reading blogs, starting with mine: TheTireMom.com. I checked her tires first and taught her how to read the Tire Halo. I could see from the way she repeated "Tire Halo" that I was on to something with that image. I smiled a secret smile. It ended up that her tires were fine.

We then drove to the school where her son, Clayton, was a teacher. School wasn't yet in session, but he was there for a meeting that had just ended. I liked him immediately. He was a devoted father of young children, supporting them and a wife who stayed home with them. The fact that he bore my Clayton's name didn't hurt either.

A walk out to the parking lot and a look at his tires revealed that, indeed, they were old and worn. He'd already done his research for his tire store, so I followed him there. A mere hour later, Clayton became tire recipient #6. This was a particularly special one. I wasn't able to buy a set of new, safe tires for my Clayton and erase the accident that took him from me. But I was able to buy a set for this Clayton. Now *that* was a gift from God. It was that tender mercy from the Lord spoken of in Psalm 145:9.

I was traveling by myself, but I didn't feel alone. I felt sustained and helped—almost as if my Clayton was cheering me on, telling me: *You can do this!*

As it happened, I would soon have to give even more credit to God for the success my mission was having. As I headed down to Georgia, where I had two appointments with friends of friends to see about candidates for gifting tires, I delighted over the coincidence that Patty's son was named Clayton. When I reached Atlanta and opened my map to see how to get to the next day's meeting, I gasped out loud. My next recipient lived in Clayton County.

I once again found myself weeping. Some of those tears were of sorrow for what I was missing. Some were tears of gratitude for the time we'd had together. The aching and the longing were still far stronger. But along with that, some of the tears were of joy at the small and simple gifts God gave me for helping me to feel connected with Clayton once more on this journey.

It turned out that my two planned tire recipients weren't ready for replacements. At only two years old, their tires looked fine even to my unprofessional eyes. I climbed back into Wolverine and thought, *Now what am I going to do?* I'd done all the legwork, I tried my best, and now I felt like it was time for God to step in.

In my prayer, I shared with God my plans to be in Alabama the next morning and how I had promised my kids that I would be safe. I pleaded for help in finding someone here in Georgia who could benefit from a set of new tires.

The name of a well-known tire store chain popped into my head. I Googled the store on my phone, found four listings, and picked the one on the right—in northeast Atlanta—seemingly at random. Even though I spent an hour in five o'clock Atlanta rush hour traffic, I knew my next recipient was waiting for me.

When I walked into the huge store, however, the thought came to me: *Not yet.*

I purchased a salad and walked back into the tire center. The tire section was empty except for a potential guy sitting on a metal bench, but he responded to my query of "Are you here to buy tires?" with "No, just getting mine rotated."

I might have sat down anyway and educated him about his Halos, but a young woman walked in and caught my eye. She was with what appeared to be her parents and daughter. Fit and strong-looking with shiny black hair, she had an air of determination and goodness about her.

I had to ask. I was more comfortable at this point in my journey talking to and educating women. That, coupled with my desire to find someone before the day was done, made me walk up to her and simply say, "Are you here to buy tires?" She responded with a yes and pulled out her credit card. "I am going to buy the tires and put them on my credit card."

I then said, "Well, can I buy you a set of tires?"

It took her several moments to answer; I was hoping that she would accept my offer.

She finally said yes. As we walked out to her car, she introduced herself as Raquel and confirmed my guess that the people with her were indeed her parents and daughter. I in turn told her about the Tire Halo and how to determine the size and type of her tires. She then took a photo so that she could convey the correct information to the tire technician.

Like most people, Raquel wanted to know why I was doing this strange tire-giving thing. On the way back into the store, I told her the story of how my husband had been killed. I was getting better at telling an automated version of my story, a practice recommended by grief counselors to detach the bereaved from the pain of the loss.

Raquel stopped me, seeming like she had something to say. She pulled out her phone, scrolled through the pictures, and showed one to me. It was a rather disturbing photo of a demolished vehicle. My hand went to my mouth to smother a cry.

"Two weeks ago," she said, "my brother survived this accident. Two other people did not." Her dark eyes bored into mine. "Bad tires were the cause of this accident."

We stood there for a few minutes, nearly frozen by amazement. Finally, she told me that her brother had called every day for two weeks begging her to check her tires. Seeing that they weren't in good condition, she'd headed for the store where we were now facing each other, still in shock at the "coincidence" of our meeting.

"I came this morning," she said, "but I discovered I didn't have my credit card. That's why I came back now."

It was a perfect example of what David A. Bednar talks about in his book *One by One.* He tells a story about a woman being available to help someone who needed her by what seemed like coincidence and asks, "Was it merely a coincidence that [she] was in the right place at the right time to minister to [a fellow sister ]? I believe that in the work of the Lord there is no such thing as a coincidence. The worth of souls is great in the sight of God."[1] It seemed to me that the Lord had also orchestrated this "coincidental" experience for Raquel and me, an experience that blessed both of us.

What Raquel wrote later in a Facebook post expressed this powerfully:

> *I remember that day I was worried about some tires. I was with my parents and my daughter, and before I stopped at [the tire store where I met Diana] I stopped in [a competing tire store], to see the prices. But something happened in my mind and I came out [...] so fast that I did not ask the prices. I left almost running and my parents behind me without understanding why[.]*
>
> *When I arrived at [the other warehouse store] to ask for the prices [. . .] I met Diana, an angel sent from heaven directly to me. I did not answer instantly [when she offered to buy me tires] because I thought I was not understanding what she was offering me, because my English is not very good[.] But when I understood what she was offering I jumped for [joy], because I knew that God had me in his thoughts and sent Diana to meet*

---

1 David A. Bednar, *One by One* (Salt Lake City: Deseret Book, 2017), 18.

> *me. For me it was more proof that God loves me and cares about me. A few weeks ago two of my brother's workmates died in a traffic accident caused by a tire and my brother called me every day [. . .] to remind me to change the tires of my car. I, always thinking about the money, could not have done it until that day I met Diana. I do not get tired of [thanking] her and God for her kindness. What a blessing. Thank you very much, Diana.*

The story of Raquel was a divine encounter. I saw that it is often through another person that God answers our prayers. As I walked out of that store, tears rolled down my face.

They were all tears of joy this time.

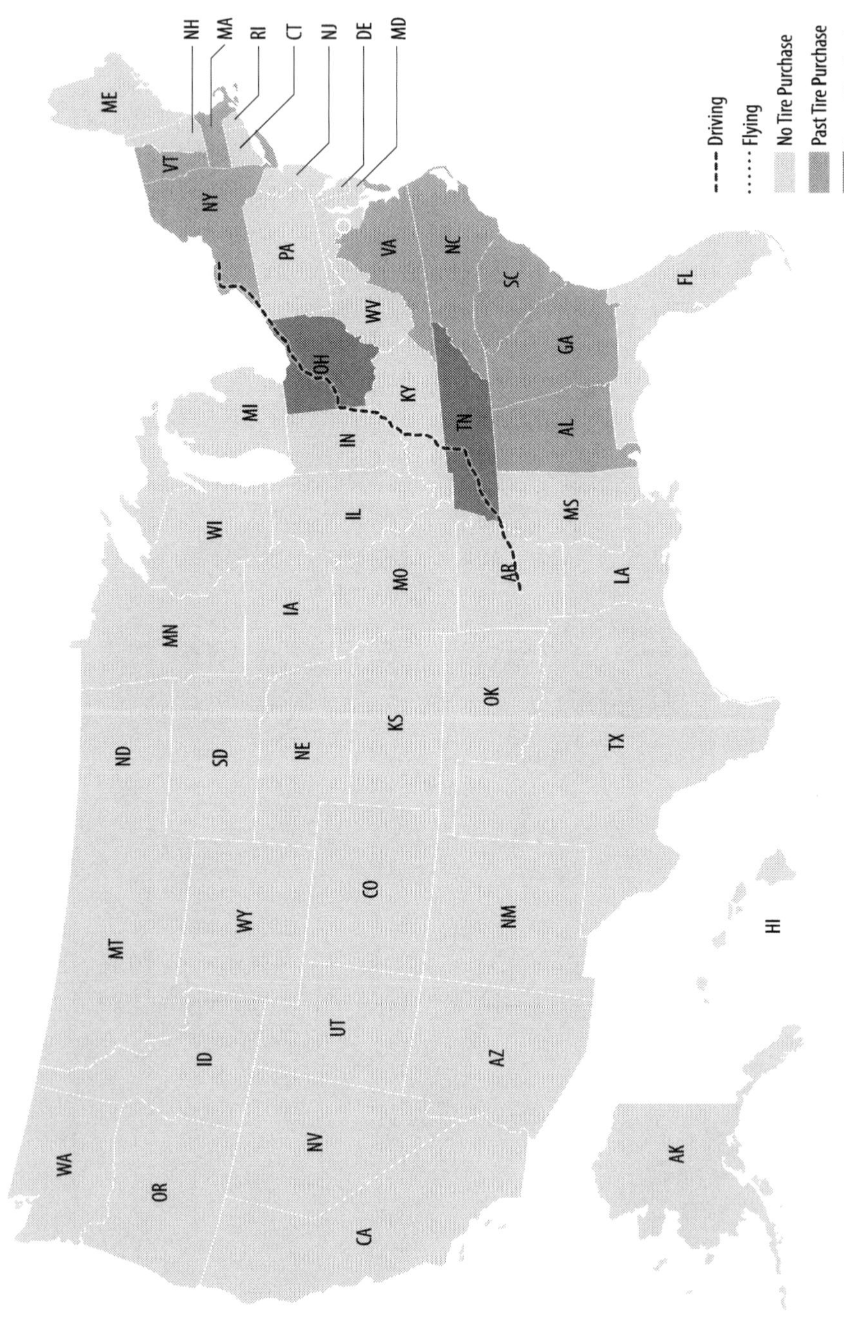


**LOOP 3**

*June 11 - June 15, 2018 (5 days)*

# CHAPTER FIVE

## LESSONS IN FLEXIBILITY

As I continued Loop 3 with my internal GPS pointing me home for June 17, I had to stop and visit Graceland in Memphis, Tennessee.

I had listened to Elvis growing up, and I had seen all his movies.

I remember when he died; now I wanted to see how he was remembered.

I had a great experience in his lavish home. It was like going back in time to the '60s and '70s because the essence of the time was captured in the drapes, the rugs, and even in the wallpaper. Looking at the pictures of his childhood in Mississippi, where he was dirt poor, I realized his was truly a rags-to-riches story.

What really stayed with me, though, were two things.

One, I marveled at how he took care of his parents and the rest of his family. No one close to him had to worry about a thing for the rest of their lives, even in light of some bad decisions that were made for him by those who were supposedly "looking out for him." His generosity touched me.

The second significant part of that visit for me was the gravesite where he and his parents were buried. The respect from not only his family but also others whose lives he touched was apparent. The long marker of marble wasn't elaborate, but the tiny statues and fresh flowers placed there, even forty years after his passing, honored his memory so tenderly. And not just his, but that of his parents. I spent a good deal of quiet time there as the water from the fountain just beyond the graves bubbled into a pool like the endless flow of life.

How people honored those who have passed on was beginning to take on new meaning for me.

From there, I headed to Nashville, which is a tourist destination for a many people, especially those who hear the siren call of country music. Needless to say, I didn't head for the honky-tonks on Broadway. I headed for a tire store, where I planted myself in line and waited. After Georgia and Alabama, this was becoming my modus operandi when I didn't have a recipient lined up, which was the case in Tennessee.

I chose a store in a well-known chain because that was where Clayton and I always bought tires. It felt familiar and safe somehow, especially as I traveled alone. I was all about being safe on every level.

I saw a man with five children enter, and realizing it was so close to Father's Day, I felt immediately excited at the prospect of gifting this father a set of new tires. The man got in line, and I followed, but a woman managed to get in line ahead of me. Feeling slightly frustrated, I eavesdropped on his conversation at the counter and overheard him say he had an issue with his tire, which were still covered by warranty. He was already being taken care of, just not by me.

Almost absentmindedly, I struck up a conversation with the woman who had gotten in line ahead of me and found out her name was Julia. It was at once apparent that this lady had that fabled Southern hospitality I was becoming so fond of.

I was at ease with Julia right away. She was very friendly, warm, and charming. I felt an immediate connection with her.

I told her my story, and all I had to see was the kindness in her eyes to know she was going to be Tire Mom recipient #9. When I made my offer, she asked in her beautiful Tennessee accent, "Now why on Earth would you want to do that?"

People always react in a big way, but Julia took it to a new level. Shocked, excited, brimming over with lottery-winning emotion, she started a mini-mission to let everyone in the store know what I was doing. I could see that Julia was a woman who loved to spread good news.

First, she told the female clerk at the register who became overcome with emotion. She told her manager, who in turn could not believe, in his words, "How cool that this is happening in our store!"

People seemed to crawl out of the stacks of tires to gather around, exclaim, and ask questions. Their words showered over me:

"This is such an amazing act of kindness."

"We want to publish this in our store newsletter."

"How about on the bulletin board?"

"Tell us more!"

As each new voice joined the crowd, I could feel myself shrinking and withdrawing. This wasn't praise I could bask in. In retrospect, I now understand why I was so daunted by the glowing attention and praise: simply put, I wasn't confident yet in my story. Yes, I'd had some time to heal, and I certainly wasn't as vulnerable as I was right after the accident, but I knew that I was in the middle of my story, my healing journey. I wasn't healed yet, I wasn't strong yet, and I was hoping the process of the journey would help me get there so that I could then someday share my story.

I had to stop this.

With my back tense and shoulders up at my ears, I found myself taking short, fast breaths. I finally raised both my hands, motioning for everyone to *STOP.* Realizing that my body language alone wasn't going to do the trick, I resigned myself to the notion that I was going to have to speak.

Right now, I don't remember my exact words. I hope they were kind. Those of us who are hurting can in turn be unintentionally hurtful with our words. What I meant to say—and what I hope I said—was, in essence, "Thank you for your kindness in wanting to share my story. But this is first of all a journey of healing. When my travels are over, I will share my story by writing it in a book. But I'm not ready to share it with everyone right now."

Julia and I talked on the phone over the next couple of days. She was in the process of telling her sorority sisters how to read the Tire Halo. To this day, we remain in contact and she continues to get the word out about tire safety. I now call her my Ms. Tennessee.

Not all instances where I trusted my gut and remained flexible on my trip ended so cleanly, wrapped in a neat little bow. There were plenty of times when I was sure I was going to find my Tire Mom candidate and it just didn't work out, or where my day turned out much differently than I had expected. These lessons tend to not be as noteworthy, but they were important to me on a personal level. There is, however, one of these experiences that I do feel is worth sharing.

There was a time when I was driving along and began to feel unbelievably tired. I pulled into a rest stop that was comfortably crowded with cars. I put my seat back and cracked a few windows for air flow and fell asleep immediately. This was something I'd done for years, even with a car full of children. I can still hear myself saying, "Okay, kids, Mom's tired so please be quiet. I need a power nap." Twenty minutes later, I'd be awake and refreshed, and after a potty break, we were back on the road again. Even on my current journey, I'd done this on every loop so far.

I woke up when my body said I'd slept long enough, and I had two realizations. One, I needed a bathroom break. Two, there were no cars around anymore. While that seemed a little odd because it was mid-morning, I only had the restroom on my mind.

Still, I scoped out the parking area, just to be aware of my surroundings. The only vehicle in sight was a huge black pickup truck parked about six spaces away. This thing was jacked up and had oversized tires and tinted windows. As I hurried toward the restrooms I thought, *Man, that truck looks mean*. Something in my gut put me on high alert.

As I returned to my car, I responded to my feeling of unease by standing taller, standing straighter, putting out my chest; I wanted to become a tough target transmitting clear "don't mess with me" vibes. I saw a small, bald Caucasian man standing between a car that had pulled up and the truck, talking to the truck driver.

I remembered my Krav Maga training:

It's always easier to avoid a dangerous situation than to get out of one.

Appear strong and determined.

Walk with meaningful steps, tall and with purpose.

I really didn't want to run unless I had to. To add to its menacing look, Big Mean Truck had clouds of smoke billowing out both half-opened windows. I pictured the big caterpillar in *Alice in Wonderland* sitting upon his mushroom smoking a giant hookah. That conversation was uncomfortable for Alice, and I knew that anything to do with that truck was not going to go very well for me.

I picked up my speed walking to Wolverine, pulled the keys out of my right pocket, and cast one furtive glance behind me to make sure no one was following me. I clicked my car fob and climbed in quickly. There was no fumbling at all as I started up the engine. Just smooth, fast actions.

Some of that confidence came from the fact that my first daughter and I had taken an evasive driving course that May. As I backed up and drove forward, having to pass behind the truck, I wondered if I was going to have to implement that training. Meanwhile, my eyes were on Mr. Truck's taillights. If the back-up lights came on, I was going to have to use the swerve-to-avoid move or even the emergency backing up maneuver.

At that point, the short, bald man I had seen earlier was still standing between the vehicles. As I drove past, we made eye contact. He crooked his figures, palm up, beckoning me to approach him.

I had the feeling that he was working with the people in the truck toward some sinister end. Over and over again, the thought came forcefully to my mind: *There is nothing in the world I can do for you.*

I sped away, got back onto the freeway, and maneuvered into the fast lane.

When I think back on this situation, my mind tells me that nothing really happened, and I feel a natural inclination towards embarrassment for what others may deem paranoia. But something deep in my gut tells me that I avoided a potentially dangerous situation.

In a book often discussed in my family, Gavin de Becker's *The Gift of Fear: And Other Survival Signals That Protect Us From Violence*, the author writes about how wondrous humans are in that they can look at their surroundings and utilize their knowledge, experience, and gut instinct to gauge a situation and make an informed decision. He also writes about how women are encouraged to please people, often to their own detriment. This sometimes causes women to adopt an apologetic tone when they are expressing what is actually an informed assessment.[1]

As men and women, we need to trust our guts and be confident in our body's ability to warn us of impending

---

1 See, for example: de Becker, Gavin *The Gift of Fear: And Other Survival Signals that Protect Us from Violence.* (New York: Delta, 1997) 210-211.

danger. We need not be afraid of offending others or hurting others' feelings when our instincts are trying to protect us.[2]

In that parking lot, I didn't know that man, and I didn't want to know that man. I just knew that I needed to get out of that situation, and I did just that.

Aside from making a vow not to sleep at any more rest stops, I thought about not only my vulnerability out on the road as a woman traveling alone but also my responses to threatening situations. Clayton had always emphasized to all of us—the children and me—that we must be situationally aware. Clayton always wanted to be safe and he ensured our family knew how to stay safe. I had relied on his expertise. However, his expertise in matters of safety did not extend to all the necessary parts of tire safety. As I progressed on my journey, I was gaining valuable new knowledge and developing strengths that would help me build on and go beyond what Clayton had instilled in our family. I was gaining more confidence and beginning to rely on myself. I put into practice skills like those I had learned in Krav Maga and the evasive driving class. That had helped bridge the gap between relying

---

2 de Becker, Gavin. *The Gift of Fear,* 1-6.

on Clayton as my protector and becoming someone who could protect herself and trust her intuition about a situation.

Most of all, I was learning to be flexible. All of us are supposed to take risks in life. If we have plans but never leave the house, we will not accomplish great things. It is only when we get out and moving, trying new things, taking risks, that we will be guided and directed.

I was learning to let that inner voice guide me, direct me, and warn me.

I pressed on Wolverine's gas pedal—and pressed myself forward.

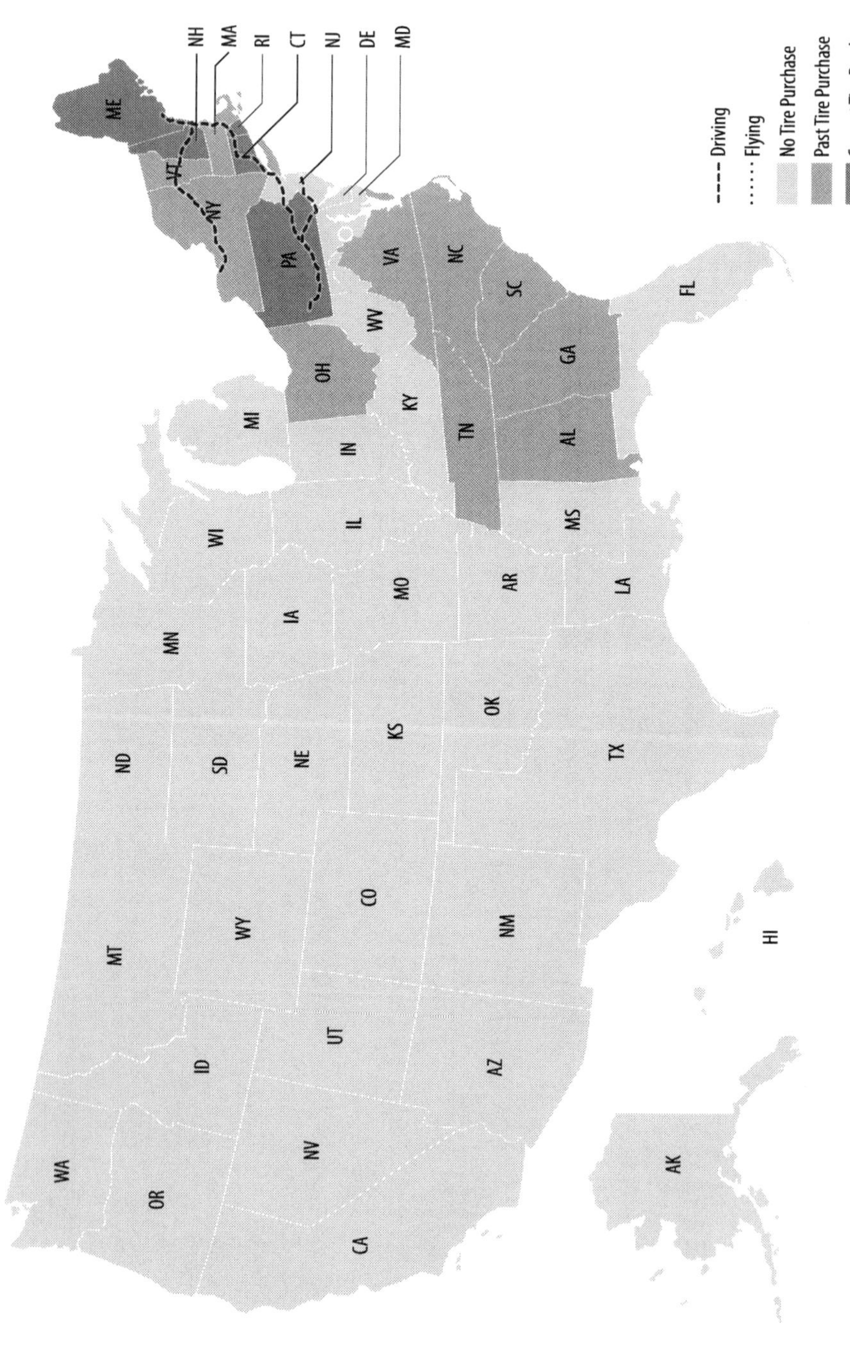


**LOOP 4**

*July 20 - July 31, 2018 (12 days)*

# CHAPTER SIX

## PUSHING DOWN THE PAIN

June was and continues to be my hardest month of the year. Toward the end of the month, both my birthday and my wedding anniversary appear on the calendar, two difficult things to get through without Clayton. But the hardest of all is Father's Day, the day in 2012 when he died.

Many people say "the anniversary of the death," but I choose not to call it that. Anniversaries are happy events. This clearly is not. Instead I refer to it as a "year mark" or say it's been X number of years since the accident. At that point, in June 2018, it had been six years.

The year I started on The Tire Mom journey, Father's Day fell on June 17, the exact date of the accident, which was all the more reason for me to not be on the road. I usually try to occupy myself with tasks and events on hard

**names have been changed to protect privacy*

days, but driving for hours couldn't be one of them. That would mean far too much time to think behind the wheel.

My time between Loop 3 and Loop 4 was about a month. It was a busy time doing maintenance around the house and attending family and social events. There was time for reflection too. I was gaining confidence in my "why" as I began by "targeting small goals and overcoming small fears that {were leading} toward {my} ultimate goal."[1]

I was chomping at the bit to get back on the road and finish the New England section of Loop 4. Though I kept myself busy when I was home with "normal" activities, the journey was beginning to feel just as normal to me.

The next states on my list were New Hampshire, Maine, Rhode Island, and Connecticut, followed by an intense week of Pennsylvania, Delaware, New Jersey, and Maryland. I still wanted to visit all the Northern states during the summer so I could avoid driving in snow as much as possible.

Everything went smoothly through New England, and I was in a good frame of mind as I headed toward Pennsylvania. My contact there was one of my college roommates I hadn't seen in thirty-six years. As I drove

1 Richie Norton, *The Power of Starting Something Stupid*, 129-130.

through New Jersey toward Pittsburgh, I hoped Margo and her husband, John, would recognize me after all these years.

Thankfully they did, and Margo connected me with Shayla, Tire Mom recipient #15. I knew at once that Shayla had recently weathered a storm in her life and was still reeling from it. That made her all the more grateful for being given a set of tires. Both of us were happily chatting as we entered the store Shayla had picked out.

And then we met our tire salesman, who I will call Mr. Snappy. Within seven seconds, I knew he wasn't exactly having a good day. You've probably run into people like him in the retail world—irritable (as if their job wasn't to help customers) and condescending. Everything about his tone said: *Why are you asking me all these questions, woman? Who do you think you are?*

This was a new experience on my journey. I guess I had been blessed with patient and instructive tire technicians up until this point.

He followed us out to Shayla's car, talking down to me the entire time, and looked at her tires. He told her she needed new ones, as if that wasn't the reason we were there in the first place. In short, Mr. Snappy wanted our money and not our questions.

Notwithstanding his negative attitude, I asked him to look at the tires I had in the back of Wolverine, hoping that despite appearances he might actually have some additional tire insight to share. In my past experiences, these tires I brought along with me helped me learn many new and interesting facts from the tire technicians I spoke with.

"I want to learn more about tires, for safety reasons. So could you look at these and tell me—"

I don't remember exactly what curt words he used to cut me off, but they were something along the lines of, "Do you want to buy tires for her car or not?"

Refusing to be put off, I tried again. "I just have a few questions for future reference."

He flippantly provided some scant details about the tires and asked us to follow him back into the store. We stood at the counter and waited while he scowled at his computer screen. He said, "We have the tires you need. For four of them that's going to cost—"

"Are they 2018s?" I asked.

He looked at me as if I had just grown an additional head. "They're '17s."

"I'm sorry, but we need 2018 tires."

With a sigh, he began to say, "Doesn't make any diff—"

This time I interrupted with, "I would like to buy my friend a set of 2018 tires."

Mr. Snappy gave me a laser glare.

"Do you have any other stores in the area?" I asked.

"Yes."

"Could you please call them to see if they have the tires we want manufactured in 2018?"

He begrudgingly helped us and we left with an address for a location that had what we needed. We climbed into our respective vehicles and drove for twenty minutes to the other tire store, which thankfully had a completely different atmosphere and the tires we requested. Within two hours, Shayla had four 2018 tires on her car, and they finished up just before closing time.

Shayla and I also had the opportunity to eat dinner with Margo and John. I learned that life had dealt Shayla some tough situations, yet she was neither bitter nor resentful. Her outlook was, in fact, amazing. I may have given her new tires, but she gave me a far greater gift by demonstrating her courage and determination to keep going in the face of adversity. This was far from a one-sided exchange.

That realization carried me as I drove to my next stop, the Flight 93 Memorial. You may wonder why I made it a point to visit places that honor those who have died. Wasn't I in enough pain? In reality, I had made the decision to pay tribute at any memorials that didn't take me too far off course on my journey. It was good to remind myself that I was not the only one who had suffered loss, and seeing the respect given to lost loved ones seemed to help me heal my own pain.

The Flight 93 Memorial honors the heroes who sacrificed their lives in order to thwart the fourth terrorist attack on September 11, 2001, by intentionally crashing the plane into a field in Pennsylvania before it could reach the terrorists' intended target. Simply driving into the park was sobering. Even while I was still in the car, I felt a sense of reverence and respect in the air. It reminded me of walking into a temple or a cathedral. I had the distinct feeling that I was here for a reason.

I parked Wolverine and was about to get out when the pain of missing Clayton overwhelmed me. Something about being in a place where so many good people had their lives cut short reminded me too much of the good man in my life whose time with our family had also been cut short. I could just imagine the wife of a man who had been on this flight getting a call from some official just as I had. Her life had been torn apart just like mine. It was like I was reliving the whole experience again. The feeling of powerlessness and despair starting bubbling up again inside me. I felt like I had the emotional stomach flu. There was this powerful physical urge to expel all of my repressed emotions. But I knew it would be messy and I wouldn't allow myself to do that there. So I forced my emotion back down yet again, not fully realizing that doing so would slow the healing process.

I got out of the car, raw with pain and grief even though I hadn't looked at a single display yet. The suffering, both mine and that of the lost passengers and the loved ones they left behind, was thick in the air. Walking toward the entrance, I continued to swallow, hard. *Don't let it come up,* I told myself. *Keep it down.*

Breathing short, fast, shallow breaths, I continued to make my way toward the memorial itself. I happen to make eye contact with a park ranger working there and he must have seen the pain in my eyes because his gaze softened and he exuded compassion and sympathy. Even without exchanging words there was a connection between us. We were human beings sharing for that moment a very sacred place where people had made a selfless sacrifice for a cause bigger than themselves. I couldn't utter a word for fear that the dam holding back my emotions would burst and everything I had been pushing down for so many years would come flooding out all at once.

I read the accounts of courage on the part of the passengers and crew. I stood for a long time in front of a quotation from President George W. Bush:

> *For generations, people will study the story of Flight 93. They will learn that individual choices make a difference, that love and sacrifice can triumph over evil and hate, and that what happened above this Pennsylvania field ranks among the most courageous acts in American history.*[2]

This quote resonated with me since I sincerely hoped that my choice to go on this trip would make a difference both in my own life and the lives of those I came in contact with.

This advice given during a time of tragedy also rang true for the tragedy that had unfolded in my life. It gave me the courage and fortitude to continue to cherish those around me and do all I could to protect others by sharing my message about tire safety.

I left the memorial feeling blindsided by how forcefully my emotions had hit me and how many times I had needed to push them down only for them to come back even stronger. At this point, I was numb and exhausted and found comfort in a dinner mostly consisting of chocolate at Hershey Park.

---

2 George W. Bush, "United Flight 93 National Memorial Dedication Address" (speech, Shanksville, Pennsylvania, September 10, 2011), American Rhetoric, https://www.americanrhetoric.com/speeches/gwbushflight93memorial.htm.

Later I wrote in my journal:

> *My heart hurts so badly. I miss Clayton. I think that maybe my pain drives me forward so that others will not have to feel this loss and [I hope to help] create a safer America. But will this crushing pain ever stop?*

Five states later, I had to say no, it would never go away. Throbbing with the agony of missing Clayton, I headed into Kentucky, and I prayed. I drove and I cried and I prayed, nothing more than a string of *Help me, please help me.* And *Will I have to live with this pain for the rest of my life?*

And then something happened. A question came to me. It flowed into me from the top of my head down to my toes. In every fiber of my being, I knew God was asking me:

*If you had healed right after Clayton's death, would you be on this trip?*

It was a yes or no question, and there was only one answer.

"No," I whispered to God.

No, I would have tried to keep living as I had been, without a thought as to how I might prevent other people from going through what we'd experienced—because I wouldn't have fully experienced it.

As soon as that resolute "no" left my lips, I felt momentarily calm. There was even a small moment of peace. There were a number of reasons for that sudden easing of the pain.

One, God had clearly heard and answered my prayer. And as He so often does, He replied with a question of His own.

Two, I was certain that I was on the correct path. I knew that now as surely as I knew my children's names.

And three, I could keep *pressing* forward. I didn't understand how at that moment, but I felt certain for the first time that there would be an end to the pain I was experiencing.

When I say *press* forward, I mean I depend mightily upon God's tender mercies, and a way is prepared for me to accomplish the task that is before me, a way I could neither imagine nor achieve on my own.

A statement by Ryan Holiday, author of *The Obstacle Is the Way*, came to my mind as I drove. He said, "The obstacle in the path becomes the path. Never forget, within every obstacle is an opportunity to improve our condition."[3]

I needed to start pressing forward through the pain. I could no longer shrink away from it. Or swallow it down. Or try to distract myself with busyness. Or

---

3 Ryan Holiday, *The Obstacle is the Way: The Timeless Art of Turning Trials into Triumph* (New York: Penguin, 2014), 7.

comfort myself with chocolate. I needed to face it and move through it.

The subtitle of Holiday's book is *The Timeless Art of Turning Trials Into Triumph.* That's what I wanted to do, but *how* to do it was another matter.

But now I was sure I was driving to that place on the distant horizon, a place of peace.

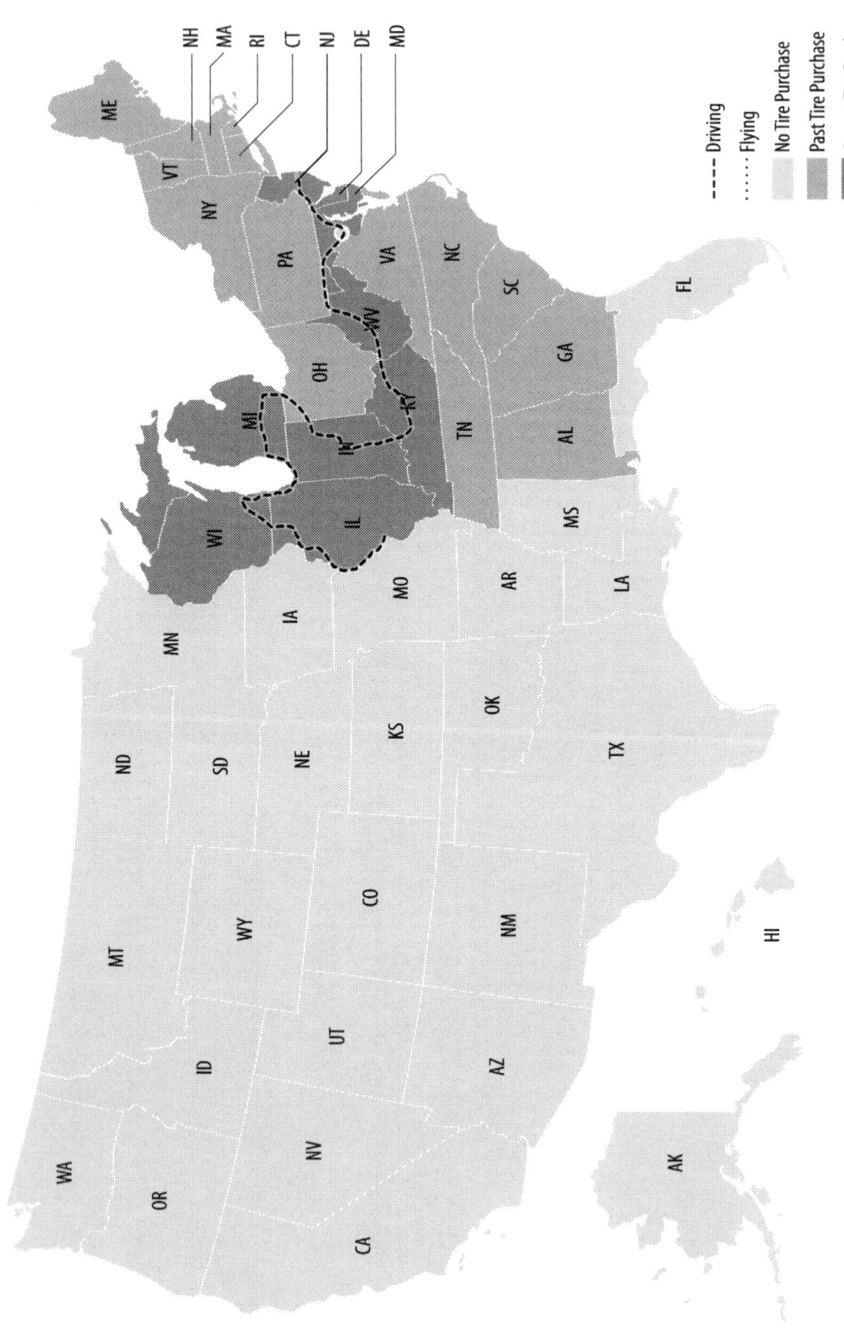


**LOOP 4**

*August 1 - August 24 (24 days)*

# CHAPTER SEVEN

## HELPING WITH A GRATEFUL HEART

When I set out on July 20, I was beginning what was to be the longest leg of my journey. I wasn't coming home until the job was almost done: a set of tires purchased in each of the remaining states except for Hawaii. There was something quite daunting about that, and I shared my concern with a friend before I left New York. "You know how you hear about marathon runners hitting a wall during a race, and they just can't go any farther, no matter how much they want to?"

She nodded me on.

"What if I get out there in Montana or Alaska and *I* hit a wall?"

She didn't hesitate before she calmly and matter-of-factly gave me her answer. "You can't go at it thinking you *don't* have

**names have been changed to protect privacy*

what it takes," she said. "You need to maintain an attitude of gratitude for what you *do* have."

My friend didn't elaborate, nor did she need to. The concept is not hard to grasp and yet I had no idea just what the benefits of enacting it would be.

On my way up to Michigan, I had been listening to the Bible from an app on my phone. I was in Genesis 50, that chapter where Joseph, known for his coat of many colors, is mourning the loss of his father, Jacob. When I read or listen to sacred text, I put myself in the situation being described and ponder how it applies to me and my life.

Although I'd read multiple times about Joseph's grief and his pilgrimage with his brothers to take Jacob's body home from Egypt, hearing the account this time it spoke to me in a way it never had before. I could see the slow movement of their caravan across the desert, and it mirrored my own. I was moving at a considerably faster pace, but my mission was in essence the same. I was trying to honor Clayton.

But was that all?

As I put the miles behind me, I went even deeper with my self-examination. How was my *whole* story going to unfold? How would it develop beyond this tire journey? I knew one thing: I could safely believe that the big picture would reveal itself. I just had to keep going.

Indeed, driving through the heartland of America soothed my aching heart, from Indiana to Michigan. It almost felt like I was going home. We had lived in Ann Arbor for five years while Clayton was getting his PhD at the Ross School of Business at the University of Michigan. Two of our four daughters were born there. We'd formed deep relationships with people there.

Two of the people we connected with there were Maureen and her husband. Maureen was particularly special to me because she introduced me to Clayton. It happened at a church dance. Maureen, seeing that I had yet to dance with anyone, came up to me and said, "See that tall guy?"

She gestured toward a young man who, unlike many, was taller than me. I nodded.

"Go over there and ask him to dance," she said.

Maureen is a persuasive person and often has good ideas, so I moved in his direction. On the way, I thought, *I don't want to just ask him*. I was thinking of how to ask him in a unique and flirtatious way. I'd seen him doing what I thought was the swing. So when I got to him, I put on my best smile and said, "Hi. I'm Diana. Can you teach me how to swing?"

He looked down at me and said, clearly and emphatically, "No."

O-kay.

I slunk into a corner and sulked. Did he have to be so rude about it?

Suddenly, Clayton was standing there, towering over me.

"Do you want to dance?" he asked.

I was so surprised that I did not know what to say. So I said, "Yes," and we walked out onto the dance floor.

Months later, when we were a couple, I asked him why he said no when I asked him to dance. He just blinked at me and said, "Well, *Diana,* you were asking me a question of skill, not of desire. You asked me if I could teach you the swing, and I couldn't because I wasn't that good at it. If you'd asked me to dance, I would have said yes."

That right there. That was why I always called him my Mr. Darcy. If you've seen or read *Pride and Prejudice*, you know what I mean. The main character was rejected by Mr. Darcy at a dance but they eventually ended up married just as Clayton and I were.

It was no wonder, then, that on my 2018 visit to Michigan, I wanted to visit the places Clayton and I had shared together. My first stop was the old townhouse where we'd lived. Touching the side of it, I remembered my friend's admonition about having an attitude of gratitude and said a quick but sincere prayer of thanks.

As I strolled around, memories washed over me. Swimming at Fuller Park with the kids. Two daughters coming into the world at the Von Voigtlander Women's Hospital at the University of Michigan Medical Center. Clayton's graduation ceremony at Rackham Auditorium, where I also attended my first Handel's *Messiah* sing-along. Hearing the bells ringing from Burton Memorial Tower. I didn't have to work very hard to feel a deep sense of gratitude for our time spent in that college town.

After I was done with my sightseeing tour, I drove to Maureen and Doug's house. As I was driving, I saw the most splendid display of the sun's rays coming through the clouds that I can ever remember. Somehow, that seemed like a good omen to me. The sight of that sunset was glorious.

As I've said before, my parents spent as many evenings as weather would allow in Colorado sitting on their porch and watching the sun go down. It occurred to me that I had been visiting places where I'd lived with Clayton and our children and also with my parents while growing up. I had experienced such goodness with both families. Not everyone gets to have that. The gratitude was palpable.

The most meaningful part of my stay in Michigan, however, was the depth of my conversations with Maureen. I could talk to her about anything, including some things that may appear to a lot of people to be negative.

It's well known that there is an anger phase of grief. Since my husband's death, I had suppressed my frustration at Clayton for leaving me with five kids and two houses in the midst of a transition that would have been messy and chaotic enough with the two of us handling it. I needed to finally work through the anger that had been simmering for so long and would occasionally boil over.

Some people had misunderstood my anger. Maureen did not. I felt safe pouring out the feelings that came with being left behind. She listened without judgment as I talked and vented about both Clayton's strengths and his weaknesses. She asked questions and I talked some more. She nudged me in the right direction and I followed. I learned the difference between sweet memories, sad memories, and hurtful memories, and that all of them were part of emerging from grief. By the end of my time with her, I felt like I had achieved resolution of some of my feelings. The anger had abated significantly, and I felt lighter.

As a result, I was a little bit more at peace when I met my Tire Mom recipient #22, a man named Gene, who had answered the call Maureen put out in her church email. She'd given me some background on him. A pastor in his own church, he also works with a Boy Scout program called Scout Reach for underprivileged boys K-5th grade. He also runs Youth For Christ, a core group for middle-school-aged kids; Families Against Narcotics, an addiction and recovery program; and a weekly food giveaway providing food for twenty-fifty to fifty families. I was happy to make the hour-long drive to the store he'd selected. He was in his fifties and graying and had an aura of selflessness.

As I watched him pick out new tires for his truck, I felt a different kind of gratitude that flowed from simply being thankful for all I'd experienced in my life. This was about being able to help someone who devoted himself entirely to helping other people. It was his turn to receive, and that made the giving mean that much more.

I had a full, grateful heart as I left Michigan and headed toward Nauvoo, Illinois. Yet the closer I got to my next destination, the more apprehensive I became. In order to understand that, a little background on Nauvoo is needed.

In the 1840s, a community of members of The Church of Jesus Christ of Latter-day Saints, sometimes called Mormons, established the town of Nauvoo, Illinois, and transformed it from a swamp into a thriving city that included a distinctive temple the Latter-day Saints sacrificed much to build. The Saints had previously been driven from their lands in Missouri by mob violence and thought they had found refuge in Nauvoo. However, after the murder of several church leaders at the hands of a mob in Carthage, Missouri, mob activity against the Saints in Illinois resurged, and some actions of the Illinois legislature convinced church leaders that they would not be protected by the government.[1] Thus, on a frigid day in February, the residents began fleeing for their lives, leaving behind their beloved city and their temple. The temple itself was eventually destroyed by arsonists and the elements, leaving a veritable ghost town on the Mississippi River.

Clayton and the children and I had visited Nauvoo several times on our cross-country road trips, usually walking down Parley Street to the river and to the site of the residents'

---

1 *Saints: The Story of the Church of Jesus Christ in the Latter Days*, Vol. 1, *The Standard of Truth*, 1815-1846. Salt Lake City: The Church of Jesus Christ of Latter-day Saints, 2018, 570-571 and 580-583.

escape. The last time we had visited as a family, Clayton and I had strolled down this trail, holding the children's hands, stopping at the little stations to read people's journal entries, which gave us glimpses into their deep and poignant feelings at their hasty departure.

I hadn't been to Nauvoo in seventeen years, and I was so looking forward to seeing the new temple, which had been rebuilt in 2002, but I was also worried. Would I have to relive my experience at the Flight 93 site? This place and the sorrowful walk to the river's edge also represented senseless death, and I was frightened at the prospect of falling to my knees in pain once more.

Yet at least I'd learned this much: I couldn't avoid the experience. I could never heal if I didn't face the obstacles in my way. So I made my way into Nauvoo, and I braced myself for an onslaught of emotion. As I stood before the glorious temple, built on the site of its predecessor, I waited for the ache and tears to resurface.

They didn't.

I was sad, of course, but I wasn't overwhelmed. Maybe they would come when I walked the path that in years past had seemed to me like a trail of tears.

Once again, I was surprised when they didn't, and here's why. When I reached the opening to the trail, I glanced at the sign and did a double take. It introduced the path as the Trail of Hope. Those refugees had lost so much of what they had, including their beloved community. Where was the hope in that?

I'd walked about ten feet in, trying to sort through that, when a blanket of hope settled over me. Years before, when my family was intact, this wretched path had seemed dark and hopeless as I imagined the men, women, and children fleeing to preserve their lives. But now, in the very midst of my own loss, I had no tears, and I was confused by that.

I couldn't decide whether to continue on by myself. Maybe I should leave well enough alone and stay wrapped in this blanket of comfort and drive away. I was about to turn back when an older couple appeared around the bend, obviously out for their morning walk. There was nothing touristy about them. They'd traveled this path many times before.

In their late sixties or early seventies, these two were in no hurry, and they stopped to greet me. I must have looked somewhere between puzzled and confused, because the lovely woman asked if I'd like to walk the trail with them.

I graciously accepted and I walked and talked with them along the Trail of Hope, which brought me more comfort than I ever imagined it would. That couple were clearly put there to see me through what could have been another horrific relapse into wretched grief. As I drove the winding road from Nauvoo to St. Louis, Missouri, the message of the Trail of Hope settled into my mind—and perhaps my soul as well.

There was hope.

There was always hope.

And I was not alone.

The doubts in the back of my mind said, "You'll never heal, you'll always be in pain," but they were fading away. In their place was a still, small voice that told me that not only was I beginning to heal from grief, I was becoming an even better version of myself. This reminded me of a religious message I'd heard that talked about an ancient Japanese art called *kintsugi*. This method of mending broken pottery consists of using gold to bind the fragments together. As a result, the cracks are highlights instead of hidden and the process creates something entirely unique and even more beautiful. During a BYU Women's Conference presentation, "Depression: More Than a Bad Hair Day, Tax Deadline, or Discouraging Moment," Amy C. Curtis a manager at LDS Family Services in Salt Lake City, said: "As an art form, Kintsugi points to valuing the history of something that has been broken and has been made whole again with a new identity. The new reformed whole [that] contains both the remembrance of what has been before and what is now."[2]

Clayton's death had broken me, but this trip was like the gold filling in the cracks of my life, and forging me into a new person that was stronger and more radiant. I used to think that everything was linear, but I was coming to

---

2 Sonja Carlson, "Depression: More than a Bad Hair Day," *Church News*, May 30, 2014, https://www.churchofjesuschrist.org/church/news/depression-more-than-a-bad-hair-day?lang=eng.

grips with the fact that we can be both sad and at peace simultaneously.

Knowing this gave me the confidence I needed to make my way into state #25.

I was nearly halfway done.

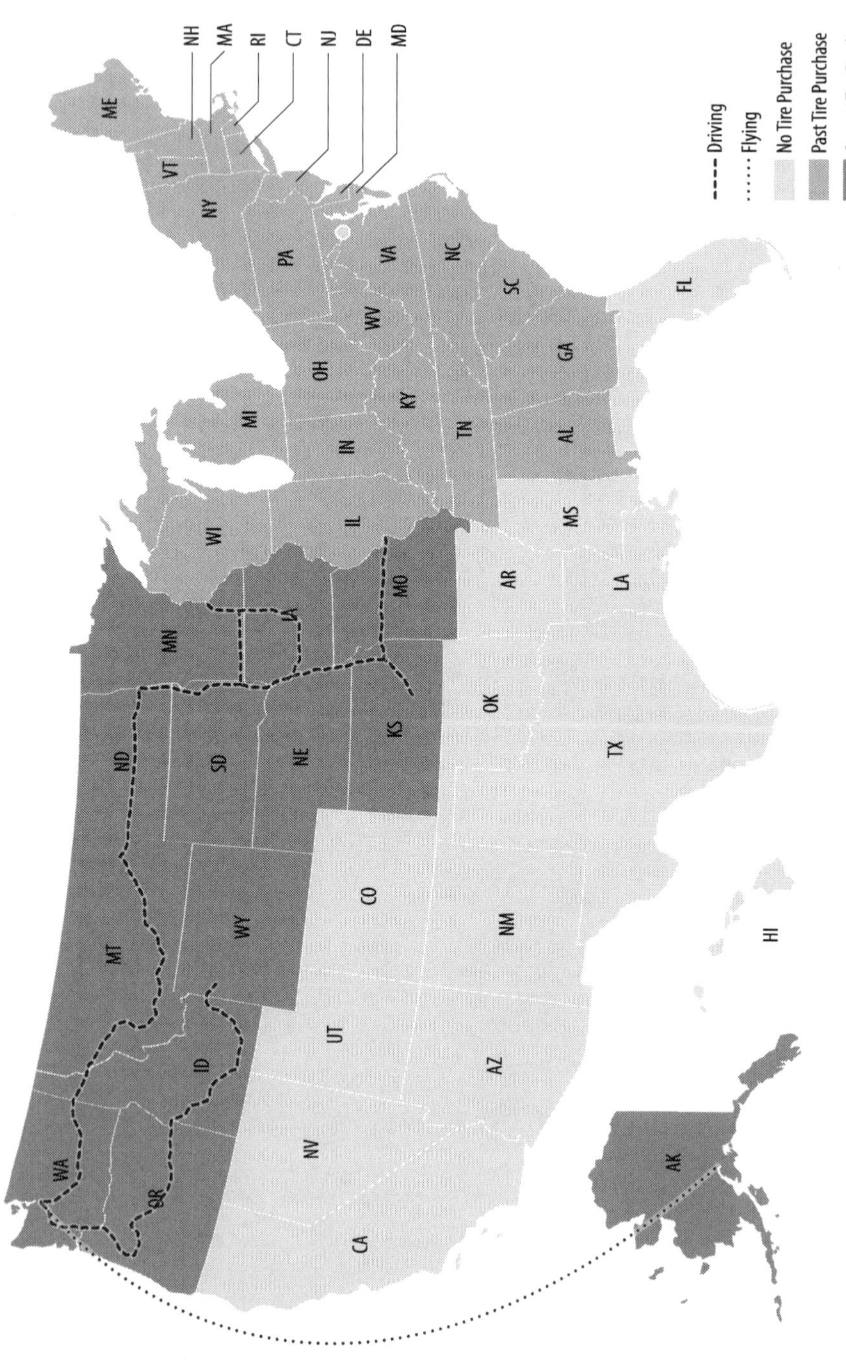


**LOOP 4**

*August 25 - September 22 (29 days)*

# CHAPTER EIGHT

## I'M NOT THE ONLY ONE

I was thirty-two states into my journey when I arrived in Washington State. That meant thirty-two sets of tires and thirty-two families blessed. I'd learned something from every one of them. But there was more to come.

I stayed with friends in Washington State, and the first night we went out for Italian food. Conversation always goes well with pasta, and that night was no exception. One of the members of our dinner party was a young man who

**names have been changed to protect privacy*

seemed very intrigued by my road trip. He had learned from my friends about my cross-country mission of buying people new tires and educating them about the Tire Halo.

It turned out that he also had a story to share. When he was just a kid, his older brother was in a serious car accident in which everyone in the van except his brother was killed. His brother was paralyzed and the tragedy was compounded by the fact that he'd just married a month earlier. And once more, it was all due to a faulty tire.

I could see the grief in his eyes still, even though it was no longer fresh and raw, and I felt the pain with him. This story helped reaffirm the importance of my mission and that my life was not the only one that had been shattered by a tire-related accident.

The next day, when I had returned to my friend's house after buying tires for recipient #32 (Anna, my sister's friend), my friend had just gotten off the phone with her father. She was white-faced.

"You won't believe this," she said.

She had told her dad about me and my mission. She'd expected an "Isn't that wonderful?" response, but instead he grew quiet. When pressed, he revealed to her that two of her cousins had died in an accident out west just two weeks before. Stunned, I listened to the account. The pickup truck they were in had veered off the road and careened into a runoff ditch and rolled onto its roof. The cause was once again a tread separation; the tire was eight years old.

Struck by how recently this had happened, I was overcome with a renewed urgency to continue sharing my message. These senseless deaths could not be allowed to go on.

The following morning was September 11, 2018, seventeen years to the day after the 9/11 terrorist attacks, I woke up thinking about the time I'd spent at the Flight 93 Memorial in Pennsylvania. Alongside those thoughts were the young man's story about his brother and my friend's about her cousins. I hauled myself out of bed, feeling heavy, weighted down somehow. But as I was getting ready for the day, looking in the mirror at my very somber face, a thought came to me.

I knew the purpose of my outer journey: to educate as many people as possible about the Tire Halo. I'd *thought* my journey was about me and my healing. But perhaps that wasn't all of it.

As you know, I think in images—tiles mainly—but at that moment I was thinking in puzzle pieces. The problem was that each puzzle piece, each accident, was only reported locally, so the people of the United States had no idea that all put together, they formed a much larger picture. What if the completed picture of my mission, like the one you see on the puzzle box, was preventing accidents on a national scale, showcasing the magnitude of the problem that was taking the lives of so many? I had been focused on sharing my personal story about losing Clayton and, although that was still important, I needed to broaden my view. I was not the only one who had lost someone. At this point it was almost starting to feel like an epidemic. People needed to understand that their car was only as safe as their tires.

Driving along Interstate 84, I could see the majestic Columbia River, and then, turning southeast, the gorgeous high plains of the Columbia Plateau. As I passed through the Blue Mountains to the Snake River along the border of Oregon and Idaho, the stunning beauty filled my soul. I had never driven through that part of the country in the daylight. It had always been dark when we made that trek in years past with the family since we would wait to stop for the night in Yellowstone.

Once again, being out in nature gave me a calm reassurance and reminded me that I now believed I had hope of being healed. I had hope that, to quote Psalms, the tender mercies of the Lord would come unto me.

I soon reached Idaho, where my fourth daughter, Camilla, was studying to be a nurse at BYU–Idaho. She became Tire Mom recipient #36—and being assured that my daughter would be safe from tire-related incidents on the road brought me great joy.

There was also another learning experience.

One of Camilla's tires was leaking. All of them needed to be the same, so I was prepared to buy her a whole new set. The tire technician told Camilla I really didn't need to do that. In his words, "I can just plug this one tire, and it should be okay."

I remarked to Camilla, "We don't do *should be okay*. Replace it."

"It could save you a lot of money—"

"No."

Camilla had her new set of tires, and I had peace of mind. *Should be okay* is not acceptable to me when it comes to safety. Even if you haven't lost someone you treasured to an accident, those words won't cover you when a tire separates from its tread and you lose control.

While Camilla was in class, I had lunch with two friends, Teresa and Donnette. The conversation turned, of course, to my mission, and I taught them how to read Tire Halos. By then I'd learned a great deal more about tires than just what was in the Halo. Some accidents are caused by faulty tire pressure. Camilla was a prime example of this with her leaking tire. There was a lot to this mission, and while I was no expert (and I am still far short of that), I was able to explain the six points of tire safety to my two friends.

That day, while we lingered over our lunch, I rattled off four of the six. "I always forget the last two," I told them. "I need to come up with an acronym."

Donnette was needed at home and had to leave, but Teresa and I continued our discussion. Teresa is one of those wonderful people who only has to hear a hint of a need before she acts on it. Miraculously, she produced paper and pen, and the two of us sat in the shade in her front yard, sipping ice water and trying to figure out something that would be memorable. Some of our attempts were fairly hilarious, but we finally arrived at something workable.

These are the basics elements of what I call **LETMAP.** It's important to know the status of your tires in each of these categories. All you need to remember is to LET the MAP guide your travels.

# Let the Map

**L**

**Lug Nuts:**
Re-torque lug nuts
50-100 miles after installing
or rotating tires.

**E**

**Examine Tires:**
Recommendations say
to check your tires
once a month.

**T**

**Tread:**
States have different
tread depth requirements.
Know your state. Be safe.

**Mileage:**
Tire mileage warranties
differ. Know your mileage.

**M**

**Age:**
Check your Tire Halo.
First two numbers = Week
Last two numbers = Year

**A**

**Pressure:**
Find the recommended
pressure inside driver's door.
Check once a month.

**P**

guide you!

**Lug Nuts** – Lug nuts keep your tire on your car. However, if they are too loose, your tire may come off while you are driving; if they are too tight, you may not be able to remove the tire easily when needed, such as when you get a flat. After you get new tires and after you get your tires rotated, the store or garage will usually ask you to return after you've driven 50-100 miles to get the wheels re-torqued, which ensure that the lugs nuts are tightened to the correct degree. This service is usually free, so take advantage of it. For remaining questions, talk to the experts.

**Examination** – Examination is an essential part of tire maintenance. Even if the other aspects of tire safety are adhered to, thorough examination might reveal an issue that doesn't relate to the other categories of LETMAP, for instance deformations.

**Tread** – Tread helps your tire grip the road and affects the handling of your vehicle. Most new tires come with tread that is approximately ten 32nds of an inch deep (10/32"). The U.S. Department of Transportation recommends that once the tread on your tires reaches

2/32", the tires should be replaced (in some states this is required by law). A convenient time to check your tread depth is when you are doing your monthly tire pressure check. The "penny test" is a common method, but there are other ways. For remaining questions, talk to the experts!

**Mileage & Warranty** – Almost every type of tire comes with a warranty that covers the tire for a specific number of years or until the tire has between 20,000 and 100,000 miles on it, depending on the type of tire. This is essentially a guarantee that you will get a certain amount of use out of the tire. Thus, it is important to record and keep track of the mileage of your tires. For remaining questions, talk to the experts.

**Age** – As I've emphasized in this book, it is dangerous to drive on old tires. Several automobile manufacturers warn drivers to replace vehicle tires after six years. You can calculate the age of your tire by finding the manufacture date inside the Tire Halo on the tire's sidewall. For example, the number in the halo might be 25/19. This means that the tire was made in the twenty-fifth week of the year 2019. Identify the manufacture dates of all of the tires on your car and write them down. For additional information on what happens to a tire as it ages, see Appendix G. For remaining questions, talk to the experts.

**Pressure** – A car's recommended tire pressure can usually be found on a sticker inside the driver's door or in the owner's manual. The sidewall of the tire lists the maximum pressure that the tire can be inflated to, which is a different number than the recommended pressure; however, it is not optimally efficient or safe to fill the tire to the maximum pressure. Check your tires' pressure at least once a month and keep them properly inflated. Don't forget to check the spare! For remaining questions, talk to the experts.

*Please* photocopy the worksheet in Appendix G and write down your tire information. It could save your life and the lives of those you love. Feel free to photocopy the info graphs in Appendices E, F, and G and keep them in your glove box. Again, all you need to remember is to **LET the MAP guide your travels**.

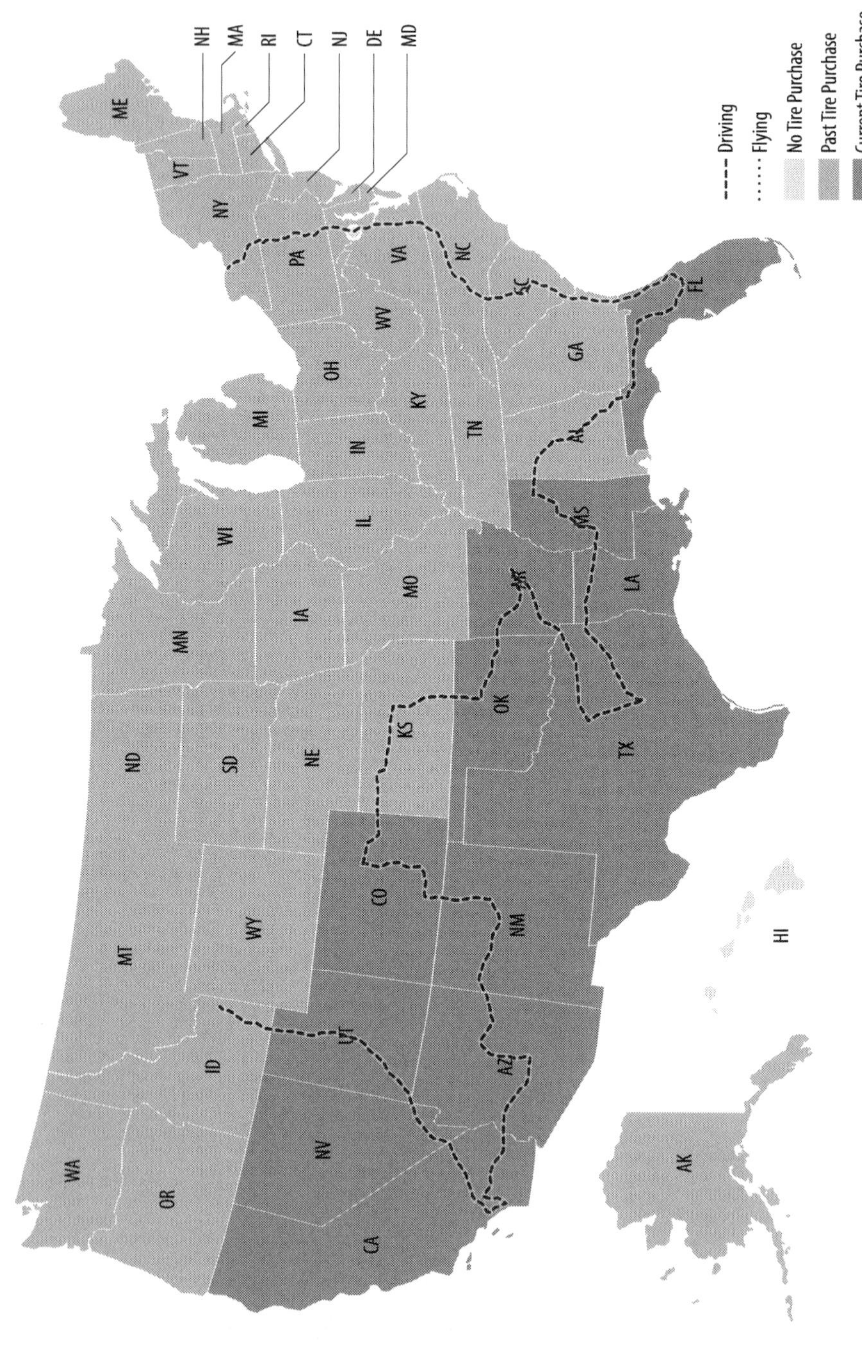


**LOOP 4**

*September 23 - October 25, 2018 (33 days)*

# CHAPTER NINE

## SANDS OF HEALING

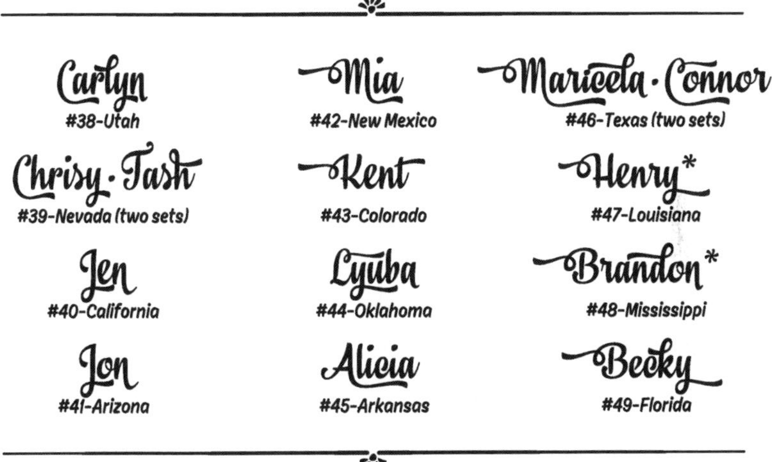


From Idaho, I visited six more states and drove up to Colorado from New Mexico. It was a soothing drive coming into the San Luis Valley during the golden hour, that time of the day when the sun rays are golden and the day is coming to a close. I spent the evening with my Aunt Frankie, and we met my brother for dinner at a fun restaurant in Salida, Colorado. After my short stay, I drove about twenty minutes east of Alamosa, Colorado, to the large unexpected pocket of sand in the San Luis Valley. The hills of yellow-brown amid the green of the mountains and

**names have been changed to protect privacy*

the sagebrush seem very out of place. These are the Great Sand Dunes, and I visited them on the final loop of my journey.

I knew the Dunes for several reasons. When I was a young girl, my family traveled all over Colorado in a Volkswagen bus like a band of hippies. One of my favorite spots was this same sandy range where we hiked and camped and entertained ourselves by gazing out the windows of the VW. These important experiences were part of the foundation for this trip. They helped shaped my love for nature and travel, particularly because the trips were when my parents were the happiest. As I stood among the dunes years later, I felt the same excitement I'd experienced as a girl—that sense of "What's the next adventure?" I had been on many adventures since then, and I was feeling like all the pieces were coming together on this most recent one. I had hope that my shattered reality might heal one day in the future.

This wasn't the first time I'd returned to the Great Sand Dunes. I went to college in Alamosa for a year before transferring to BYU–Provo to earn my degree in Recreation Management, and the Dunes were very much a part of that experience. Later, when I was pregnant with my second daughter, Clayton and I brought Celesta to this wonderful national park, where I had once shared my childhood memories with Clayton. There is something almost magical about seeing a place you love through the eyes of a person you love.

As you know by now, whenever I went back to places he and I had been together, I waited for the resurgence of emotion I felt at his loss. This time, as I explored the part of my past that mingled with the sand, not only did the pain not resurface, but I felt, for the first time, peace and calm wash over me. I was pleasantly surprised by the fact that this visit was not so much a peek into the past as it was a completely new experience.

After soaking it all in and purchasing my usual souvenirs, I headed south, driving in the shadow of the mountains. To my right were the western plains. As the morning sun rose, its light seemed to race across them toward me. The gold-coin aspen leaves were alive with that light, so alive that I could almost hear them tinkling against each other like tiny bells. Then, with the stunning beauty waking up the world, I was struck.

Not with overpowering loss or wrenching pain, but with the magnificence around me. I found myself deeply grateful. Not simply thankful that I wasn't in pain, but genuinely appreciative of the gifts of the moment. It was a turning point I had not expected.

I'm not sure how I covered the next hundred miles. You know that moment when you realize you've been driving but you don't remember steering or braking or shifting because you've been so lost in your own thoughts? This was one of those times. Wolverine was basically on autopilot, taking care of the external journey while I focused on my internal journey.

An image came to me. I saw and felt tiny drops of life-giving water soaking into the roots of a tulip starting to blossom after a long difficult winter, and I knew they'd been making their way there since the very beginning of my journey.

A nourishing drop of God's unfathomable creation here, another drop of sweet contact with my roots there, still another from each deep and satisfying conversation with a beloved friend over there, even more refreshing drops with each visit to a temple, and one giant drop for every time I gifted someone with tires and watched the tension ease from the recipient's shoulders.

Now, leaving the Dunes behind, I saw in my mind's eye that with each drop of rain, the tulip grew taller, stronger, and more beautiful, not just remaining in the ground where it was safe from the storms that *might* come.

I knew that I wasn't there yet. Maybe I would never fully heal, but I was making progress and it felt great. The quiet strength and beauty of the West spoke to me as it had to Teddy Roosevelt. Teddy had gone west to North Dakota to soothe his grief, and even though I was driving my Suburban over the open plains of the West instead of riding a horse, we had both come here on journeys of healing from the loss of someone we loved.

There is more significance in these many experiences than I've perhaps been able to express, so let me go a little deeper. Before Clayton's accident, I had such expectations, such big plans for our future as empty-nesters. Three of our children were off on their own and two were ready to launch when he passed away. We were going to travel, serve, and love. When he was killed, I had to let go not only of the present Clayton but also of the future one as well. Releasing either one meant giving up on those dreams.

But they were pieces of *my* life as well. I had dreams of my future self, of who I wanted to be and what I wanted to do. One thought that had plagued my subconscious and broken through to the surface so many times these past six years was *Who am I without Clayton and our life together?*

I went even deeper into that thought as Wolverine put mile after mile behind us. When Clayton was in charge of a university congregation at church and our children were growing up, I was the giver. That was my role, and I embraced it without question and loved it. My role on this journey was an extension of that role as I gave people tires and shared information, hopefully saving lives. It was a good and spiritual way of living.

Now, though, experiencing the palpable excitement of stunning vistas and the continuing drops of healing rain, I had to learn to be a receiver. Not just a willing recipient of the gifts God was offering me, but a gracious one.

We've all been in the situation where you buy someone a treat or bring them a present for no real reason, and that person says something like:

*No, I can't let you do that. Let me buy yours.*
or
*You shouldn't have done this. Really, it's too much.*

Doesn't it sap the joy of giving right out of you? You want to shout: *Why can't you just say thank you?*

I'm thinking God might say that countless times every day, at least to me. Giving is a good and joyful thing. Receiving is as well, and it requires nothing but a gracious response. As I pondered the important balance of learning to both give and receive graciously, I was overcome with gratitude for all who had given graciously to me.

There were the kind people who had lent me support at the Flight 93 Memorial in Pennsylvania and the Trail of Hope in Nauvoo, Illinois. The sweet couple who provided the funds so I could get home after my first failed attempt on this journey. My children, whose wise encouragement kept me from hauling a VW Bug and trailer all over the country. All of the tire recipients who graciously received my gifts of tires. They were such an example to me—not only of gratitude but also of trust in a complete stranger. And finally a loving God who had shaped the Great Sand Dunes and the many sun rays and sunsets throughout my journey and the aspen leaves that rang like little bells, which had been a catalyst for my healing.

Somewhere between the dunes and Denver, I surrendered. Though my hands were firmly on the wheel, internally I held them up and said, "Clayton is really gone. I have to let go of him until we see each other when my life here is over. I'll be okay."

In the same way that I'd just experienced Great Sand Dunes National Park in a new way, I had to live my life on a different path than the one I'd dreamed of for so long. I had to be willing to receive as well as give, or my tank would eventually be empty.

Six morc states and the corresponding gifts of tires later, I arrived home to Rochester on October 25, 2018. I was feeling elated. I had driven to all of the lower forty-eight states by myself. Wolverine boasted 153,095 miles on his odometer, which meant that I had driven 32,455 miles. Forty-nine people had been given new, safer tires. I had flown to Alaska when I was in Washington state, and I had only one more state to go.

My final stop would be Hawaii—after I first spent a week sequestered in a cabin in Western New York, where I had laid the foundations of what would become this book. Just me and my journal and computer. No worries, no interruptions.

On November 1, 2018, I received a phone call from the friend who was taking care of my three dogs. Balto was not doing well, and she was taking him to the vet.

Let me give some background. I have three dogs—Balto, Sandy, and their son, Jack. Balto—with his tuxedo-like markings, signature pug curly black tail, and Chihuahua head and ears—is the clear alpha and a doting husband to his wife, Sandy, with her white terrier/Shih Tzu fur that to us seems like a wedding dress to Balto's tuxedo. As a family, we had created an entire story around their relationship, and they were officially part of our family.

When I got word that Balto was on his way to the vet and it could be serious, I dropped everything and raced from my writing retreat near Niagara back to Rochester, where I found him gravely ill. He was diagnosed with idiopathic thrombocytopenic purpura (ITP), which is an attack by the immune system on the blood platelets. Sandy was diagnosed with the same condition a few weeks later. They were given medication that would hopefully put them into remission, but the vet made no promises.

Even the most casual of pet owners knows the anxiety that comes from that kind of situation, and I was more than a casual pet owner. However, there was another layer to my anxiety. This situation triggered flashbacks of receiving the news about Clayton's accident. At this point, my heart jumped every time I saw a call from a phone number I didn't know.

I know that people and animals are different, that my attachment to Balto and Sandy, strong as it was, couldn't compare to my deep love for Clayton. But loss is loss, whether it's a job, a house, a relationship, a reputation, your health, or a season of life. Some losses are more profound than others, but each one affects us with some level of anguish. You'd think that once you've suffered an extreme loss such as the death of a husband, subsequent losses would pale in comparison. So yes, I knew what to expect emotionally if Balto and Sandy passed away. However, each new loss brings back those feelings of hopelessness, and perhaps even terror, and compounds them. Every time.

After the loss of Clayton, I was never the same, and I knew this loss would change me as well. I understood that eventually Balto and Sandy and even Jack would die. Dogs have a short life span. But I wasn't ready at that point to let go of the comfort and the joy those animals had provided for me when I was home alone.

Balto and Sandy did go into remission and are still creating platelets to this day. Our little dog family remains intact. A month after this dog health crisis, I was able to return to my plan and head for Hawaii, the final state on my journey.

What new experiences waited for me there?

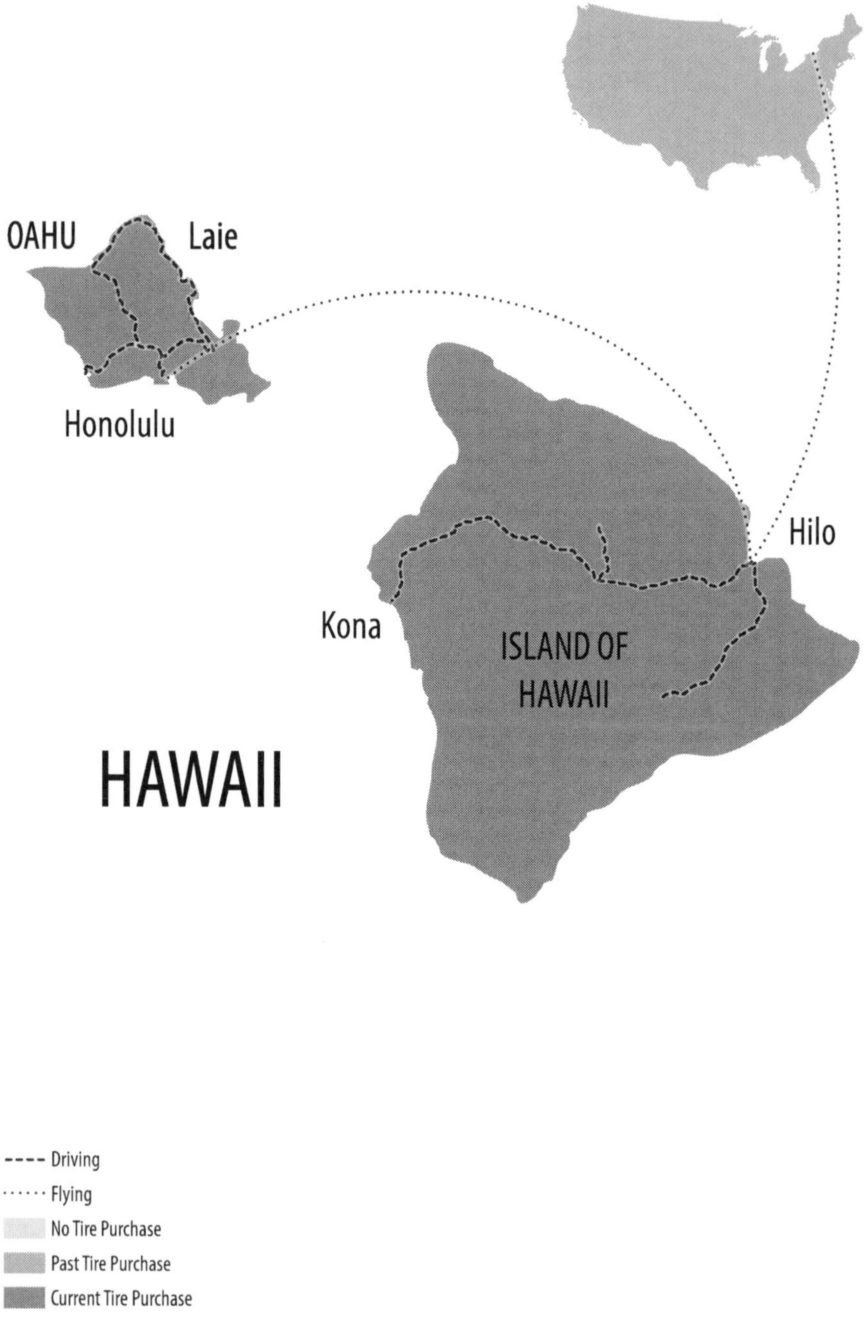

OAHU
Laie
Honolulu
Hilo
Kona
ISLAND OF
HAWAII
HAWAII
Driving
Flying
No Tire Purchase
Past Tire Purchase
Current Tire Purchase

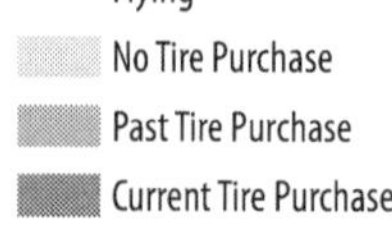

**LOOP 5**

*November 26 - December 7, 2018 (12 days)*

# CHAPTER TEN

## WAVES

### Erie

***#50-Hawaii (regifted to one of Clayton's students)***

Going back to Hawaii was a major step for a couple of reasons.

First, it was the last state on my journey and represented the achievement of my goal: fifty states and fifty tire recipients.

Second, Hawaii was the last place Clayton and I had lived together. I'd been back a few times since his death, but only for a brief vacation with a few of my younger children and a graduation. This would be the first time I would be by myself and stay for longer than I had to, and that meant facing some things I had yet to deal with.

Here's what you should know about our life in Hawaii before the accident. Clayton had a great job at BYU-Hawaii. Our children were growing up to be fine individuals. I was even taking a few college classes to learn some new skills. All of us, it seemed, were developing as people—and what lovelier place was there to do that than on the Hawaiian Islands? We took full advantage of the slower-paced lifestyle. Clayton and the children and I moved so much. There was no "perfect place," and each location had its benefits and its challenges. But in Hawaii we felt we were in the right place at the right time and our future seemed bright.

As I've mentioned, at the time of Clayton's accident, I was at our house in New York, where my in-laws were currently living, and where I was downsizing and putting some of our belongings in storage so we could sell our house there. When I returned to Hawaii several weeks later, my whole world had changed, and it felt as if I had left our dreams in Hawaii.

As I flew over the Pacific, I felt apprehensive. Despite all the growth and healing, the questions gnawed at me: *What kind of grief was waiting for me in Hawaii? Was I healed enough to withstand it? Or would I regress and lose all the ground I'd gained?*

It took me all day to fly to Hilo, Hawaii, where my sister-in-law Patricia and nephew Daniel picked me up from the airport. Reuniting with them kept any difficult emotions from surfacing, and since Clayton and I had lived together on a different island, there weren't as many memories here. The next day, my brother-in-law Eric went with Daniel and me to the tire store, where I bought Eric new tires for his truck. I loved ending the mission with a family member, and I knew Clayton would be pleased with this choice. Clayton was the oldest of three boys. Growing up, he had always been their protector and tried to help them where he could. His brothers were his best friends. Moreover, Eric used his truck to help people out in the rural areas of the Big Island. His well-worn tires meant his truck regularly got stuck in muddy, unpaved roads. Hopefully, that wouldn't happen as much now.

As it turned out, Eric was able to pay it forward by giving the truck with the new tires on it to a family that could really use it, and one of the parents had taken classes at BYU-Hawaii from my husband, Clayton. Talk about coming full circle!

Happy as I was, paying for that fiftieth set of tires was a bit surreal. Was I really done? Was this truly the end of this part of my journey? I was so used to thinking *Who will be the next tire recipient?*

But as I flew into the Honolulu Airport on the island of Oahu, something else filled my mind: the last time I saw Clayton alive was at this airport.

The last time I hugged him.

The last time we kissed.

The last time I felt protected by this man whose soul and mine were so entwined.

As I walked through the airport now, I had to pass the exact spot where we last held each other. I took in a long breath, and I waited. If there was ever a place where I had to be ready for sudden a surge of emotions, it was here.

But it didn't come.

Rather than feeling relieved, I was puzzled. *Where was the grief?*

I didn't have time—or maybe I didn't take time—to examine that. I had only five days to visit as many old friends and teach as many people as I could about the Tire Halo. It was basically a marathon. I was still on a mission. The buying was done. The teaching was not.

The day I left Hawaii, I took one last walk on the beach. I was physically tired but emotionally nourished. I felt loved and appreciated and grateful. Noticing the details of God's creations had become second nature to me by then. I looked at the shoreline and focused on the patterns of the waves crashing on the sand. The ebb and flow of the water rushing out to sea and then immediately coming in again created designs that surpassed those of any human artist.

The memories of our time here seemed to flow with the shallow waves. I could picture our family walking our normal Temple Beach route, Clayton always in possession of a walking stick, one of the many he crafted while we lived there. He used them to ward off stray dogs, but they constituted another sign of his protection for all of us.

I felt a calm peace, and my eyes drifted further out to sea. It was time for one last swim.

As I entered the water, the waves hit my legs, and I was caught off balance. I steadied myself and continued walking into the waves. As the waves got bigger and began hitting my torso, it became harder to keep my balance. Constantly steadying myself, I pushed through to the calm, rolling, open ocean. I dived down into the warm salt water and swam into deeper water, just as I'd done so many times in those happy years. But something was different now.

After swimming for a while, I turned around and watched the waves as I bobbed in the water. The experienced ocean swimmer knows that you should always keep your face toward the waves. Show your back to a wave and it will knock you flat on your face. I realized that until recently, I had approached my grief like an inexperienced beachgoer. I had suppressed it, turned my back on it, and as result, it had knocked me down, again and again. As I felt the rhythm of the waves, I realized that you can't turn your back on grief. I hadn't begun to heal until I had finally turned around and faced the waves of my grief head on; I had to confront it and learn to keep my balance as the waves hit, again and again. The words of Ryan Holiday came back to me: "The obstacle is the way." The experience of riding or diving into each wave of grief molds and shapes us. It pushes us from negative to positive, from pain to greater empathy and understanding.

I swam now with a new sense of excitement, out past where the waves were crashing, where the water was calm. I knew when the time came, I could ride the waves back to shore. I appreciated the lesson of healing the brutal waves had taught me, and I could help others swimming the rough seas of grief get out past the shore where the water is more serene.

Back on the beach, I wrapped a towel around me and looked out at the Pacific again. One more thing stood out to me. The waves that hit the sand used their power for good too. Their force knocked the rough edges off the debris that had been washed out to sea and was now being washed back to shore. The rocks and driftwood came back from their sea-tossed journey smoother, their rough edges worn off, ready to become a precious trinket or a sturdy walking stick.

Could it be that the purpose of the waves of sorrow and grief was to wash away the jagged and angry emotions? Might it also be possible that the receding ones allowed the good and grateful feelings to surface?

I sank into the sand and worked that through in my mind. Facing the hard-hitting waves of grief had dulled many of my sharp edges. Now the memories that rose to the surface were smooth and precious. I had also made new memories of the time spent with friends and family and people I met over tire purchases who would now always be a part of me. I could also see the many ways God had carried me, leaving only His footprints in the sand.

I had no doubt now. I was healing.

You will notice that I didn't say I was healed. An old injury always requires special care. Just as the waves on this beach never stopped, neither would this process. Not just of becoming whole again but of being more than I had ever been.

I left Hawaii later that day, having received a downpour of life-giving rain. I was going home with a deep sense of accomplishment. As I watched the sun set from my window seat on the plane, I basked in the feeling of fulfillment and completion. Looking at the sunset drew my eyes to the horizon, and my thoughts to the future. Looming in the distance was my next mountain to climb.

**"GIVE ME THIS MOUNTAIN"**
*-Joshua 14:12*

# EPILOGUE

I've been climbing mountains since I was a young girl growing up in Colorado. I was surrounded by them, and I had a father who loved to climb them. I felt that I had to be right there beside him, so at age fourteen, I almost made it to the top of the Middle Teton in Wyoming with my brother and my dad.

After becoming a more experienced mountain climber, I had better luck at age seventeen when the three of us took on Mount Olympus in the state of Washington. It's the highest and most pronounced of the Olympic Mountains of western Washington state and is recommended only for experienced mountaineers who have glacier travel and crevasse rescue skills and gear.

This time, I made it to the peak with my father and brother and stood there in wordless wonder at the view of the range and beyond. People who didn't climb could only see Olympus buried deep in the center of those rugged mountains from 5,242-foot-high Hurricane Ridge.

I was seeing Mount Olympus from up close. I was on it. And I loved it up there.

By then I had become my father's main climbing partner, and our adventures together took us all around Colorado. Armed with ice axes and crampons, we made our communal way up many a steep slope, sharing experiences that allowed me to communicate with my dad in ways I probably wouldn't have without that common interest. Unbeknownst to me, though, I was developing another relationship at the same time. My parents weren't religious, and at that time, I had very little concept of God. But every time I summited another mountain, I was more and more aware not just of the beauty that surrounded me but also of the power behind the creation of that beauty. I simply had no idea at the time where that soft whisper of awareness would take me. The feeling that these views gave me helped me realize there was a God when I started becoming religious in my late teenage years.

I didn't climb many physical mountains after Clayton and I were married and started our family. I was climbing the mountains of laundry, food preparation, and wholesome recreational activities. We climbed these mountains as a family. In the summer of 2014, two years after the tragedy that took my husband's life, when I was living in Virginia with my two youngest, I felt the urge to climb some physical mountains again. My two youngest children, Camilla and Gerrit, were on board, so we trained together. It was a lot more difficult than when I was seventeen. The three of us made our way up Mount Marcy, the tallest mountain in New York, and Mount Washington in New Hampshire, the highest on the East Coast. At the end of August, over five glorious rain-free days, we made our ascent up Mount Olympus. Following our guides, we warmed up on our twelve-mile hike at sea level through the Hoh Rain Forest. Then we actually started climbing. The next five miles took us to Glacier Meadow, at 4,200 feet, where we spent a short night. At 3 a.m., we left Glacier Meadows to climb up the lateral moraine, over the Blue Glacier, up the Snow Dome, over and through two passes and up a steep snow face, finally reaching the summit by roping up and climbing up the rock wall face to the top. We basked in the glory of the stunning 360° view of the world on that gorgeous sunny day. We had made it to the top at 7,979 feet. You may be wondering what on Earth all this talk of mountaineering has to do with my journey as the Tire Mom.

While the kids and I were planning and training for our Mount Olympus adventure, I got to thinking about how much courage and strength was required to climb that scary mountain as well as the ones we'd already conquered. I felt I had enough of those qualities to summit the physical mountains; I just didn't feel that brave and strong on the inside to climb the *figurative* mountains: the endless grief, the emotions that so often knocked me down, decisions I now had to make alone, not just for me but for the children I still had at home.

I also felt I couldn't overcome my fears of writing, especially the process of actually writing and promoting a book. Those were mountains too. Yet somehow, I *was* working my way up their steep, rugged sides.

In the next few years, I made it to higher inner peaks where my view was less obstructed by raw sorrow and deep fear. By 2018, as you are now aware, I knew there was a big mountain I had to climb. This was the journey you've read about.

I thought as I embarked on this quest that I would simply gift a set of tires to someone in every state. I had no idea that such a climb had things to teach me, not just about giving but about receiving. Everyone who agreed to accept my gift—some of them after some heavy persuasion—did so graciously. From those people, with their heartfelt thanks and their grateful bear hugs, I learned that that is the kind of gratitude that I can give to God. It has occurred to me that every time I paused on my journey to gaze at a shimmering lake or stand in awe of the sacrifices memorialized across the country, I whispered my thanks to God. And every time, I was blessed even more.

I know that God wants me—and all of us—to receive happiness. God wants me to be healed. God wants me to accept that grace. God wants me to see that I am an individual, and my recovery will continue to happen in a way that's uniquely right for me—just as someone else's journey out of grief and into a new life will be designed especially for him or her.

Yet the principle is the same for all of us. I call it the Three H Principle, and I discovered its power for myself as I implemented it on my journey.

First, we are Hurting from some type of loss.

Then, we reach out and Help.

Finally, as we help, we start to Heal.

How that is implemented will be specific for each of us. We will all have different mountains to climb.

I wasn't done once my mission was complete. It became clear not long after I set out on my journey that I was going to write a book. I had expectations of posting on a blog and on Facebook over the course of the trip, and maybe even starting the book somewhere out there, so I kept a careful journal and wrote in it diligently—but I wasn't able to truly start until my journey was complete. By the time I got to the end of a day of driving or meeting people and going through the emotional experiences that awaited me everywhere I went, I was spent.

So even though I knew that my next mountain of writing a book was out there on the horizon, I couldn't climb that one until the first was conquered. My job on my journey was to get the message out by focusing on my goal as The Tire Mom. That message was far more important than trying to do everything at once. To put it bluntly, I had to let go of my ego and do only as much as I could realistically accomplish at the time. Lives were still being saved. When I was ready for the next climb, that mountain would still be there.

Obviously it was, because you are holding that book in your hands. The mountain has been climbed, but I didn't do it alone as you'll see when you read the acknowledgments. More and more ego set aside. More and more focusing on the message rather than on me. More whispers from God that I am to gratefully receive His gift of happiness even as I continue to give.

There is at least one more mountain on the horizon for me to climb. I can't see its shape clearly yet. There are still clouds obscuring my view. But I do know it has something to do with continuing to get the message about the Tire Halo and LETMAP out to as many people as possible. You can help me climb that mountain by sharing these important messages with those you love and help prevent further tragedy. As for me, I will be climbing that mountain along with you. Thank you all for joining me on my highway to healing.

# BIBLIOGRAPHY


Ballard, M. Russell. *Counseling with Our Councils: Learning to Minister Together in the Church and in the Family*. Salt Lake City: Deseret Book, 2012. Kindle.

Bednar, David A. *One by One*. Salt Lake City: Deseret Book, 2017.

Bush, George W. "United Flight 93 National Memorial Dedication Address." Speech, Shanksville, Pennsylvania, September 10, 2011. American Rhetoric. https://americanrhetoric.com/speeches/gwbushflight93memorial.htm

Carlson, Sonja. "Depression: More than a Bad Hair Day." *Church News*, May 30, 2014. https://www.churchofjesuschrist.org/church/news/depression-more-than-a-bad-hair-day?lang=eng.

de Becker, Gavin. *The Gift of Fear and Other Survival Signals that Protect Us from Violence*. New York: Delta, 1997.

Holiday, Ryan. *The Obstacle is the Way: The Timeless Art of Turning Trials into Triumph.* New York: Penguin, 2014.

Hubner, Clayton. "Dr. Clayton Hubner." YouTube video, 40:26, posted by BYU-Hawaii Learning Channel. https://www.youtube.com/watch?v=o6waoTFNM44.

Hubner, Clayton. "To Live a Life Worth Losing." Devotional, Laie, Hawaii, October 4, 2011. BYU-Hawaii Speeches. https://devotional.byuh.edu/index.php/node/1726.

Lindbergh, Anne Morrow. *Gift from the Sea* (New York: Pantheon Books, 2005).

Norton, Richie. *The Power of Starting Something Stupid: How to Crush Fear, Make Dreams Happen, and Live Without Regret*. Salt Lake City: Shadow Mountain, 2013.

*Saints: The Story of the Church of Jesus Christ in the Latter Days.* Vol. 1, *The Standard of Truth, 1815-1846.* Salt Lake City: The Church of Jesus Christ of Latter-day Saints, 2018.

"The Life of Theodore Roosevelt." National Park Service. Last modified October 9, 2014. https://www.nps.gov/thri/theodorerooseveltbio.htm.

# APPENDIX A:
## ACKNOWLEDGMENTS

I could not have made this book without the help and support of so many people.

As a person who grew up not liking to read or write, I've been guided throughout this amazing process.

I've grouped these wonderful people into what I call my "Tire Mom Hall of Fame."

---

Athens, who created my amazing logo. Melissa, Nancy, Marilyn, Carlyn, Parker, and Celesta who thoughtfully wove this tapestry of words from my verbal accounts into a coherent written story. You have been such a blessing in my life! Also, a big thank you goes to my proofreaders Leeann, Richie, and Steve. To Nina, who accepted my challenge and made it happen, and Raquel, your final touches are so appreciated. Brandon for transforming my words into graphs and pictures that helped support my ideas. This journey was made possible by each of you sharing your gifts and talents with me. I will be forever grateful for the efforts of each of the members of my Tire Mom Hall of Fame!

---

Celesta, Carlyn, Christina, Camilla, Gerrit, Parker, Jonah, Marlene & Eric, Don, Penny & Kent, Frankie, Bill & June, Eric & Patricia, Mark & Brenda, Bernie and Marlene, DJ & Deanna, John & Sandra, Rick & Barbara, RJ & Iris, Herb & Annie, Scott & Lisa, Joann & Karl, Mark & Vicki, Chris & Cindy, John & Leeann, Nell & Wes, Andrew & Keela, Marylynn & Jordon, Sharon & DeRay, Holly & Dan, Andrew & Julie, Jolynn, Adrian, Andrea, Chris, Julie, Tony, Kathy, Stephen & Gigi, Clyde, Bryant, Bruce, Heidi, Jarolyn & Collin, Dan & Karla

Ron & Patricia, John & Mele, Connie & Riley, Doc & Madelyn, Lois and Don, Erin & Matt, Steve & Margaret, Kim & Sue, Max & Donna, Teresa & Kevin, Donnette & Glade, Bishop & Liz, Eric, Caryn & Brian, Tammie, Saralyn, Leeann, Bonnie & Lenard, Elise, Richie & Natalie, Marlyn & David, Jennifer & Keith, Marty & Cary, Susan, Beth, Alisa & Joshua, Marcus & Mirian, Heidi & Dan Audrey, Lilia, Tetua & Rod, Laurie, Keaka, Lena, RosieMaria, Beth, Keith & Debra, Julie & Brian, Doug & Ginny, Brian & Nicole, Bob & Suzy, John & Kay, Kim & Frank, Karen & Jeff

Bill, Steve, Tina, Randy, Jim, Liz, Leslie, Jesica, Kim, Jodi, Dan, and Cherly

Marcia, Eileen, Annabel, Deborah, Jaimee, Kayla, Jen, Linnea, Patti & Brand, Marcia, Patty, Clayton, Raquel, Becca & Ty, Julia, Janet, Maura, Candi, Paul and Katherine, Brenda*, Patricia*, John & Margo, Shayla, Debbie, Mike & Mike, Jennifer, Mark*, Jeff, Meera, Maureen & Doug, Gene, Paula, Laurel, Gloria & Sam, Lisa, Becky, Angela, Dow & Diana, Elena, Keith, Jan, Negash, Penny*, Bill*, Don*, Bob, Beth & Hank, Mak & Clan, Eric, Anna, Hattie, Jim & Ann, Kyle, Matt, Liz & Oluf, Dora & Family, Camilla, Laura, Ida Beth & Larry, Dalton Clan, Carlyn & Parker, Chrisy, Tash & Eric, Lynda & Bill, Julia & Jen, Jon & Allyson, Mia, Kent, Lisa & Grant, Quinn & Tab, Luba, Robin, Alicia, Linda & Craig, Maricela, David & Donna, Dave, Connor, Dawn, Henry*, Brandon*, Lee, Sheri, Becky, Michelle, Bruce, Kevin, Adam, Dr. Koch, Samantha, Shannon, Nicola, Christine, Samuel, Evelyn, RoxMary & Abi

Angel, Dawn, Hollie, Kerry, Jolene, Sarah Lee and Courtney, Leann and Eli

Joy, Olga, Jennifer, Mindy, Eva, Julia, Tricia

Julie and Ron, Ann & Guy, Ken, Sid, Jake, Devin, Steve, Angel, Chris, Wanda

Cary & Suzy, Nathan & Shala, Jennifer, Debra, Heather & John, Zion & Bryce, Maria & Charlie, Brandon & Sarah with Henry, Lorna & Gordon, Dorothy, Staci & Max, Karen & Carl, Katie, Claire & Frank, Steve, Elisabeth & Greg, Karen and Brent, Karen & Dan, Linda & Larry, Pat & Gary, Joween, Melanie, Doug, Eunice, Anna, Edna, Hirit, Emma, Joann, Melanie & Zack, Deborah & Darren, Chandee & Nick, Mary, Nick, David & Betsy, Hope & John, Linda, Janet, Amy, Brian, Frank & Lynae, Cheryl, Cindy, Stephanie, Sara & Jeff, Tom & Nancy

Jaimee, MaryAnne, Joann & Chuck, Alissa & Jonathan, MariLouise, Trista & Brad, Katrina, Danielle, Chloe, Anniken & Gary, Lue, Tate, Eleanor, Kelsey & Garrett, Seleta & Brett, Michelle, Alex & Margaret, Wende & Kurt, Marilyn & Peter with Zekiel, Christie Sue & Adam, Gail, Kathy, Silvia & Jim, David, Lee, Lisa, Bill & Barbara, Marilyn & Mike, Marcia

Kristian, Barbara, Hildi, Amber, Abri, Cindy, Mark, Ann, Elena, Dow & Diana, Laura, Erika, Alissa, Vanessa, Kayla, Laurie, April, Renee, Katie, Monica, Tanya, Christy, Keith, Logan, Alayna, Bruce, Amber, Anniken, Jan, Elizabeth, Sally, Bob, Deborah, Julie, Andrew & Andee, Liz, Jaquita, Randall, Jolynn, Michelle, Regina & Alfredo, Mary, Nell, Laura, Kim, Gretchen, Zack, Donna, Sarah, Marsha & Mike, RC, Amy, Carolyn, Sherry, Serena, Whitney, Keela, LeAnne, Shadow, Ella, Heidi, Brittany, Dan, Jolene & Ed, CJ, Erika, Jarolyn, Melanie, Morgan

**names have been changed to protect privacy*

# APPENDIX B:

## William Clayton Hubner, Jr

1958 - June 17, 2012, Father's Day

# THE SUPER STAR

## OUR FAMILY TRADITION

I want to share with you one of our family traditions that we practiced and still do when we are together as a family. It began as a lesson Clayton taught all of us when our children were little. We were living in Wisconsin, and our brood of five was at that age when they bickered and found fault with each other at the slightest provocation.

With his usual wisdom, Clayton found a long-term solution. I mentioned in the book that my husband was a garage sale aficionado. One Saturday morning, he came home with a single plate that didn't match the rest of our dinnerware. I raised a questioning eyebrow, but when he explained his plan, I was all in.

Each night at dinner in the days that followed, the odd plate would show up at the place of one of the family members. That meant that person was the Super Star for the meal. After eating dinner together, we went around the table, and every person had to say something he or she loved about the Super Star. Negative positives, like saying, "I love the red spots on your face" when a sibling was having an acne breakout, were forbidden; compliments had to be genuine and positive. As receivers, the children also learned how to graciously accept the compliments with a simple, "Thank you."

With that done, then the Super Star had to say what they loved about themselves. Jesus taught that one of the great commandments is to love your neighbor as yourself. When we love ourselves, we'll find it easier to love others.

The whole ritual would end with a cry of "All for one and one for all!," and the Super Star would then pick a cheer. It could be "Huzzah!" or even blowing raspberries—repeated three times. When international students joined us for dinner—as they often did—they taught us cheers from their cultures. Our kids learned to hoot and holler in a number of different languages.

That wasn't all they learned. Sometimes when company came to the house, the visitor would get the Super Star plate. Thus, the children would have to make conversation with them before dinner so they could discover something they loved about the person. As a result, they grew up learning how to interact comfortably with adults and to look for the positive in people—and perhaps most important, to say thank you for the blessings that came their way.

# TO LIVE A LIFE WORTH LOSING

BY CLAYTON HUBNER

*DEVOTIONAL GIVEN OCTOBER 4, 2011, AT BRIGHAM YOUNG UNIVERSITY*

Brothers and sisters, *goedemorgen*!

I love the beautiful tradition that we practice here at BYU-Hawaii, of having a replied greeting from the group or congregation. The same tradition, in one form or another, is present in many other cultures throughout of the world. Accustomed as you are to now-familiar words of greeting like "aloha," "mabuhi," "talofa," "kiora," "iorana," "malo e lele," "bula vinaka," or others, I'm sure that when you first heard me speak, you may have thought that I was loudly clearing my throat. But what I just said to you is "good morning" in the language of my Dutch ancestors, and if you were adventurous enough, you said "good morning" back to me in the same language

Although I have lived here in Hawaii for more than eight years, I am nevertheless the son of Celts, Vikings ,and Barbarians. Like many of you, I am descended from ancient warrior societies, albeit ones from much colder climates—with Russia, Mongolia, and China being notable exceptions. But we have all been called here to the Gospel Family, and more specifically to Laie by a message of peace. Many of my ancestors were seafarers who plied the world's oceans in search of fortune and glory, or perhaps just looking for a warmer place to live. In this regard, I again feel a kinship with those of you from Asia-Pacific, a part of the world with a rich history of epic voyages, over land or over sea, in search of that which is precious.

The Savior clearly understood the world of commerce and travel because he referenced it in his parables. In Matthew we read: "Again, the kingdom of heaven is like unto a merchant man, seeking goodly pearls: Who when he had found one pearl of great price, went and sold all that he had, and bought it" (Matt. 13: 45-46). The price of the pearl reveals its great worth in the eye of the beholder, for he was willing to sell everything else that he had in order to possess it. Surely he had been actively searching for a long time for a pearl that was so special, and in the intervening years he had become wise in the ways of commerce and in the value of the many gems that were offered in trade. But this one pearl stood out among all the other "goodly pearls" that he had examined. His well-trained eye recognized its inestimable worth, and he willingly sacrificed all else to make it his. This story reveals a very important truth: the knowledge and blessings of the gospel cannot be had cheaply—they will require "all that we have," if we are to possess them. Nothing can be held back in this transaction, and all that remains for us will be this one pearl of great price, with nothing else to distract us.

The history of the human race is a history of explorers, and adventurers, individuals who were brave enough to leave familiar shores and to venture beyond known horizons in search of something better. We are born with an insatiable curiosity and a desire to discover, to learn, and to know. Human history is a tale of movement and migration, of facing dangers and overcoming obstacles. In a very real sense, it is an apt metaphor for our journey through mortality, for we are sent here by a Heavenly Father so that we can learn to walk by faith, to gain experience, and to be proven worthy to stand again in His presence and thereby to receive the rich inheritance that he has prepared for us before the foundation of the world. He does not send us into this world unprepared; every person is born into this world with the Light of Christ that gives us knowledge of good and evil. And if we are faithful, we will be able to hear the whisperings of the Holy Spirit, who after our baptism and confirmation can become our constant guide and companion throughout our life's journey, helping us to discern truth from error, teaching us all things that we should know, bearing witness to eternal truth, and serving as a conduit for essential inspiration and personal revelation.

It would be nice to be able to report that all epic journeys and adventures have happy endings. If this were the case, no one would feel any hesitation when venturing into the unknown. However, too often our paths are fraught with risk and danger. While the rewards are great, the risks are great as well. Before the modern era, many a traveler left the bosom of his or her family, never to return again. With such great uncertainty, departures were often sad affairs. Likewise, homecomings were especially sweet. In the interim the traveler was left to their own devices or the wisdom of their traveling companions when it came to coping with unexpected perils encountered along the way. To have any chance of returning home, it was important that the traveler not give up hope, no matter how difficult the challenges that they faced.

It is an important part of human nature that we feel bound to cling tenaciously to life, no matter how difficult the circumstances that we face. For this reason, we are buoyed up by stories of survival that illustrate the indomitable human spirit. This will to live is essential if we are to pass through the trials that are an essential part of our mortal probation. Necessary as well is a strong drive to take care of our own needs. While we cannot hope for gain if we cling to safety, we also naturally eschew those conditions or circumstances where our life would be at risk. And it is something counterintuitive, rare, and sometimes quite wonderful when someone is willing to lay down their life for another or in the pursuit of a higher goal. But that is one of our noblest human attributes: self sacrifice for a higher purpose. It is at the heart of nearly all deeds of great heroism, and it is also at the core of the atonement of Jesus Christ. "Greater love hath no man than this, that a man lay down his life for his friends" (John 15:13).

The call to embrace the gospel fills our lives with hope and purpose. The Savior said, "I am come that they may have life, and that they might have it more abundantly" (John 10:10). In following his perfect example and his commandments, we are blessed in this life and the next, for "he who doeth the works of righteousness shall receive his reward, even peace in this world, and eternal life in the world to come" (D&C 59:23). With so much to live for, it seems paradoxical for us to be taught that we must lose our life if we are to have any hope of saving it. Before resolving this matter, let us consider further the subject of losing our life.

Next week I will have the opportunity to go to the House of the Lord in order to perform sacred temple ordinances on behalf of a cousin who did not live long enough to complete these for himself. His life ended tragically in the company of a supposed friend early one cold, wet autumn morning, when the car he was riding in careened off the road, hit a telephone pole, and then was literally ripped in half when it slammed into a tree. Members of his extended family would like to believe that my cousin died instantly, since the injuries that his body sustained were too horrific to describe. It was no longer a fit or sustainable tabernacle for his spirit, and thus a merciful God allowed his mortal probation to come to an end there amidst the dead leaves and litter at the side of a road in the hilly midlands of Staten Island, New York.

While I am in no position to judge him, I fear that my cousin was still woefully unprepared when his life ended. He had experienced a very tempestuous and violent youth, and his adulthood was marred by perverse and even satanic practices that he encountered and too frequently embraced when he wandered into forbidden paths and became lost. Nevertheless, he and I stayed in touch over the years and we conversed frequently on the phone or via email. I had grown up viewing him as a wayward younger brother, born out of season and out of context, who should have been an heir to the blessings of the gospel had things worked out differently for him. Despite his many incorrect choices, I was not ready to abandon him. As time passed, we spoke with increasing frequency about gospel-related topics and about the purpose of our life here on Earth. In small but consistent increments I could see his heart softening, and I was quite confident that one day, with the Savior's help, he would be strong enough to turn away from his sinful past and enter the waters of baptism. I had looked forward to that day, had prayed for that day, and had worked toward that day. When I was a young man, I had made a promise to my grandmother that I would not forget my cousin nor would I fail to stay in contact with him, no matter how troubled he might be or how much trouble he might find himself in. I'd like to believe that I kept that promise while my cousin lived, and by completing his temple work, I shall continue to keep that promise now that he has passed beyond this life.

The Savior taught: "Thou shalt live together in love, insomuch that thou shalt weep for the loss of them that die, and more especially for those that have not hope of a glorious resurrection. And it shall come to pass that those that die in me shall not taste of death, for it shall be sweet unto them; and they that die not in me, woe unto them, for their death is bitter" (D&C 42:45-47).

My cousin lost his life, based in part on his own choices and, more specifically, as the direct consequence of the driver of the car in which he rode being incapacitated by drugs and alcohol. That man now faces many years in prison as a result of his choices and their tragic consequences. I do not believe that my cousin was ready to leave this life so soon, but I do believe that he had already reversed his fall and was moving with increasing speed in the right direction.

Many years prior to my cousin's death, my own life was nearly forfeit as the result of a boating accident. When I was eighteen years old, I took part in a white water rafting trip on the magnificent Green River in northeastern Utah. With the river swollen by fresh snow melt and by an icy surge of water released from the base of the Flaming Gorge Dam, it promised to be a fast-paced, adrenaline-pumping adventure—just the thing that every young man dreams of!

Unfortunately, the adventure nearly cost me my life. Inadequate training and poor communication between our crew caused us to get badly hung up as we passed through some particularly rough rapids. A series of bad decisions by panicking raft-mates resulted in my suddenly being catapulted from our vessel into the river's 40° water. I was immediately caught in the powerful flow of a chute where water raced between two large boulders and then sucked me into an underwater hole or hydraulic that spun me around until I nearly ran out of breath.

Bruised and disoriented, I eventually surfaced many yards from the raft and was again caught by the swift current that violently dragged me through the rocks and obstacles of a long series of white water rapids. When I finally saw a chance to escape, I tried to swim for shore; however, my extended struggles and the extremely cold water had completely sapped my strength and caused my muscles to cramp and seize up. Even when I somehow managed to get near the safety offered by the bank of the river, I could neither stand up, nor could I grab onto anything in order to save myself. The river's strong current tugged at me relentlessly and then carried me away again into another series of rapids.

I could no longer swim and only the limited buoyancy of my flimsy life vest now kept me afloat. Many minutes passed with no relief in sight as I tried to find my way through the foaming white water. All the while, I could feel the ice-cold river sucking the life from my body as my core temperature plummeted and I went into hypothermia. "So this is how it's going to end for me?" I remember thinking to myself. Through no fault of my own, it seemed that my mortal life would soon come to a close in the frigid waters deep in that beautiful canyon. Well beyond both shivering and any sense of numbness, I remember feeling very peaceful and sleepy, too tired to fight anymore and too spent to call for help from a raft I saw further down the river.

As the chill current carried me onward, I noticed that the people in that downstream raft had seen me, helpless and motionless in the water, and they had changed course and were paddling back upstream in my direction. Several anxious minutes passed as we neared each other. Finally, when I was right next to the raft but unable to even hang onto its side, willing hands and strong arms reached into the icy river and pulled my very cold and near lifeless form into the safety and warmth of their craft.

My cousin lost his life as he careened out of control down a dark and winding roadway. I nearly lost my life adrift and helpless in the icy rapids of a raging river. Surely this cannot be what is meant by losing our lives in order to find them. How many people in this world are careening through life, spiritually lost and out of control? How many more are adrift in life's river, their will to hang on slowly slipping away due to the cold indifference of our telestial world? Where are the willing hands and strong arms that will reach unhesitatingly into the frigid water to pull them out? Where are the disciples of peace who would bring purpose and calm to a life that is directionless and out of control?

Three of the New Testament gospels teach a very unique doctrine of self-sacrifice that foreshadows the doctrine of consecration, which is taught more fully in the scriptures of this dispensation. In Matthew we read: "For whosoever shall save his life shall lose it and whosoever will lose his life for my sake shall find it" (Matt. 16:25). Likewise, Mark conveys the same principle with only minor variation: "For whosoever will save his life shall lose it; but whosoever shall lose his life for my sake and the gospel's, the same shall save it" (Mark 8:35). Luke recounts the Savior presenting the same doctrine on two different occasions. In the first instance he teaches: "For whosoever will save his life shall lose it: but whosoever will lose his life for my sake, the same shall save it." Later, the same principle is taught again: "Whosoever shall seek to save his life shall lose it; and whosoever shall lose his life shall preserve it" (Luke 17:33).

While all of these scriptures clearly mention one losing their life in order to find it or in order to save it or preserve it, there is a strong connection between them and the parable of the merchant who gave all he had in order to acquire the pearl of great price, meaning the gospel and its offer of life everlasting. This mortal existence, and the time that it affords us, along with our agency, are really all that we have that is of any enduring value. Yet each of these scriptures tells us that this—all that we have—is the cost of discipleship. If our own life is all that we have to offer in exchange for the blessings of eternity, then it behooves us to live a life worth losing for Christ's and the gospel's sake.

Immediately prior to sharing this doctrine, of losing our life for Christ's and the gospel's sake, the Savior taught: "If any man will come after me, let him deny himself, and take up his cross daily, and follow me" (Luke 9:24). By exercising self-control and sensible self-denial, and by keeping the commandments on an ongoing basis, we purify our lives and make them worthy of sacrifice as we seek to follow the author of our salvation. In this way, we are giving him our best self, that which worthily shows our everlasting gratitude for his Atonement and for the Father's plan of happiness.

The animal sacrifices offered by ancient Israel were required to be unblemished and without spot (see Numbers 28:9, 11, etc.). They were to be the "first fruits," the very best that could be offered. Only this would be an acceptable sacrifice. This same pattern was followed when Heavenly Father allowed His firstborn and only-begotten son, who was sinless, without blemish or spot, to be offered as the only acceptable sacrifice on our behalf as Atonement for our sins.

When we lose our life for Christ's and the gospel's sake, we are presenting it as a willing sacrifice. If we would follow the pattern established in Scripture, a life worth losing can only be the very best life we have to offer, one that is as pure and as sanctified and holy as we can make it. It is not the leftovers or cast-off bits. Were we to liken this to meat, it would be the prime cuts of our time, our talents, and our treasure, not the undesirable, mangled scraps that are usually swept up and made into hotdogs or turned into dog food.

This is the only way that we can truly follow the perfect example of our master, who taught: "Therefore, what manner of men," and I might add, women, "ought ye to be? Verily I say unto you, even as I am" (3 Nephi 27:27). This means that his law must be our law, and his values our values. Not only must we be willing to lose our lives in order to follow him, we must also fully and openly reject the corrupting values of the world, since we cannot serve two masters (see 3 Nephi 13:24). This need to make a choice is presented very clearly in the Joseph Smith translation of Matthew, where we read: "Break not my commandments for to save your lives; for whosoever will save his life in this world, shall lose his life in the world to come" (JST Matt. 16:27).

The Book of Mormon, in Mosiah 11 through 17, recounts the story of Abinadi, a faithful man of God who had lived a life worth losing and who was sent among the people to prophesy of their impending destruction unless they repented of their sins. Abinadi's plainspoken condemnation of their wickedness angered the people as well as their king, who commanded that Abinadi be brought before him so that he could be put to death. However, the Lord delivered Abinadi out of their hands before they could harm him.

Two years passed, and then the Lord sent Abinadi back among the people to deliver the same unpopular but essential message. Abinadi once again trusted in the Lord; however, he must have also known that his life would be forfeit if he was caught because he came in disguise. When the time was right, he made himself known, and moved upon by the Holy Ghost, he spoke with great boldness, urgency, directness, and clarity. The people were again angered and offended, and they captured Abinadi and carried him bound before the king. There, Abinadi withstood their cynical, self-serving questions and accusations and he confounded them in their words, condemning them for perverting the ways of the Lord.

Although the Lord had previously delivered Abinadi from harm, there could be little doubt in his mind that the end of his own life was near. When the enraged king commanded that he be carried off and slain, Abinadi forbid the king's servants to lay their hands on him, for he had not yet delivered his message. They dared not touch him, for the Spirit of the Lord was upon him and Abinadi's face shone with an "exceeding luster," the same as Moses's did when he conversed with the Lord on Mount Sinai. He spoke to his captors, these corrupt leaders, with great power and authority from God, reminding them of the commandments and testifying of their iniquities and condemning them for failing to teach the people.

Abinadi bore witness of Christ and called the wicked king and his priests to repentance. Surely there would be no miraculous deliverance for him this time. The truth of Abinadi's words would be sealed with his death. In keeping the commandments and in fulfilling the mission that the Lord had called him to do, Abinadi had truly lived a life worth losing. One cannot doubt that his sacrifice was acceptable before God, and that his final plea, as the flames consumed him, "O God, receive my soul," would be granted by a loving and grateful Heavenly Father. In being willing to lose his life for Christ's and the gospel's sake, Abinadi had found life everlasting. But it wasn't just his life that was saved. One of the king's priests, a man named Alma, had been moved to repentance by Abinadi's testimony and had fled into the wilderness, there to re-establish the true church and to teach the gospel to all those who would believe.

The prophet, Joseph Smith, and his brother Hyrum also lived lives worth losing. Having done all they could to "take up their cross" by living the commandments, and having done their very best to do God's will in this life despite persecution and great adversity, they willingly went to Carthage in late June of 1844, knowing their lives would be forfeit. They easily could have fled across the Mississippi River to Iowa, but they chose instead to go peacefully with their captors, like lambs to the slaughter (See D&C 135:4).

Long before his martyrdom at Carthage, Joseph had chosen to lose his life in Christ's service and for the gospel's sake. John Taylor would later testify that "Joseph Smith, the Prophet and Seer of the Lord, has done more, save Jesus only, for the salvation of men in this world, than any other man that ever lived in it. In the short space of twenty years, he has brought forth the Book of Mormon, which he translated by the gift and power of God, and has been the means of publishing it on two continents; has sent the fullness of the everlasting gospel, which it contained, to the four quarters of the Earth; has brought forth the revelations and commandments which compose {the} book of Doctrine and Covenants, and many other wise documents and instructions for the benefit of the children of men; gathered many thousands of the Latter-day Saints, founded a great city, and left a fame and name that cannot be slain. He lived great, and he died great in the eyes of God and his people; and like most of the Lord's anointed in ancient times, has sealed his mission and his works with his own blood; and so has his brother Hyrum. In life they were not divided and in death they were not separated!" (D&C 135:3) He declared that "the Book of Mormon, and . . . Doctrine and Covenants . . . cost the best blood of the nineteenth century to bring them forth for the salvation of a ruined world . . ." And of Joseph and Hyrum he further testified: "They lived for glory; they died for glory; and glory is their eternal reward. From age to age their names go down to posterity as gems for the sanctified" (D&C135:6).

Both Joseph and Hyrum were ordinary men. But through faith, repentance, by following the commandments, and with God's help, they had done many extraordinary things. They forgot themselves and lost themselves in the service of the Lord and the gospel and eternal shall be their reward.

Losing our life, for Christ's and the gospel's sake, is the only way for us to find life eternal. Though Abinadi, Joseph, and Hyrum literally gave their lives, in the end, to seal their testimonies, the less dramatic but even more compelling part of their examples is what they did day by day in putting the Savior and the gospel first in their lives and in laying aside their own self-interest. This is a pattern and a type that each of us can follow as we give up our lives that we might know the Lord, and as we follow His commandments and His perfect example of service and selflessness.

The Joseph Smith translation of the New Testament sheds further light on the importance of not just losing our life for Christ's and the gospel's sake, but also of being willing to lose our life while at the same time living the gospel through service to our fellow man (see Mosiah 2:17). Luke 9:24 reads: "For whosoever will save his life, must be willing to lose it for my sake; and whosoever will be willing to lose his life for my sake, the same shall save it" (JST Luke 9:24). Likewise in Mark we also read: "For whosoever will save his life, shall lose it; or whosoever will save his life, shall be willing to lay it down for my sake; and if he is not willing to lay it down for my sake, he shall lose it. But whosoever shall be willing to lose his life for my sake, and the gospel, the same shall save it" (JST Mark 8:37-38). The power of this principle lies not only in our losing our lives for Christ's and for the gospel's sake, but also in our willingness to do this, whether or not that ultimate sacrifice will be required from us.

Through personal revelation and the whisperings of the Holy Spirit, we can know what the Lord would have us do in his service as we willingly surrender our agency and subjugate our will to his. In this way, we lose our life in his service day by day as we act as worthy instruments for good in His hands.

Sometimes we are called to serve in small and simple ways. As we learn to hear and to be responsive to the whisperings of the Spirit, and as we learn to discern between truth and error, we may sometimes face circumstances where following the inspiration we receive might seem inconvenient or even counterintuitive. Nevertheless, if we would truly lose ourselves in the service of the Lord, we cannot fear man more than God (D&C 3:7), and we must press forward with faith and diligence in obeying His word.

I recall many times as a young missionary in the Netherlands when I would receive a prompting from the Holy Spirit to strike up a conversation with someone on the train or on the street corner. Sadly, I too often doubted the inspiration that I received, and I feared men more than God and kept silent. On one occasion, the Spirit quietly told me to talk with a man who was sitting next to me on the tram. I doubted this inspiration, and thought in my mind, "If this is really the Holy Spirit, then what should I talk to him about." To this I was given the answer, "Ask him if he has a son named Tom." Again I doubted, and fearing embarrassment and humiliation, I remained silent. In quiet reflection later that day, I was ashamed of my lack of courage and faithlessness and I saw how my efforts to lose myself in the service of the Lord had suffered as a result.

Then something happened one cold winter night when my companion, Elder Kruger, and I were looking up referrals in an old, badly run-down neighborhood near the harbor in Amsterdam. As was our custom, when the referral turned out to be a dead end, we decided to do some tracting for a little while so that we could count the time toward our twenty-hour-per-week proselyting quota. Since I was the senior companion, what happened next falls squarely upon my shoulders. I approached a door and was ready to ring the bell when the Spirit clearly told me, "Do not go to that building; leave the area immediately." I was frustrated by this, because we were already behind in our tracting hours, and without knocking on a few doors, our trip to this faraway part of town would not count toward our quota. Again, I doubted my ability to receive personal revelation and I feared man more than God. In this case, I worried that the Zone Leader would be upset that we did not reach our quota. So I ignored inspiration and rang the doorbell. It was my turn to run to the top of the narrow, unlit stairway to give the door approach, while Elder Kruger waited on the stoop below. We were never out of sight of each other, and we were only a short distance away. I had been in many ancient, unlit hallways as a missionary, but this one filled me with a strange unease. At the top of the steep flight of stairs, I turned to my left and saw a figure standing in a dimly lit doorway down the hall. I introduced myself and said that we had a message about Jesus Christ. The man spoke just two words to me: "Get out." But they were said with such darkness, evil, and malevolence that my blood ran chill. I said "Okay." Once again the Holy Spirit spoke to me, with great force and urgency. It said: "Run."

This time I listened, and I needed no further encouragement. I literally flew down the stairs, surprising Elder Kruger when I hit the bottom. "Run," I said. And that's exactly what we did. He did not question my command. We ran for nearly a mile in our heavy coats that bitterly cold night. When we finally stopped, wonderful, obedient Elder Kruger asked, "What happened back there?" I related to him my impression and disobedience, and then the Spirit's clear command to run. Elder Kruger said that one second he saw me at the top of the stairs and then next I was at the bottom. And he also saw a man coming right behind me, chasing after me! This I had not seen, since I was too busy flying down the stairs.

The idea of what could have happened to me and my wonderful companion, for whom I was responsible, struck me like a heavy blow. As I have prayed to understand that experience and to learn from it, I have no doubt our lives may have hung in the balance. I resolved then and there to lay aside my fears and my foolishness, to stop trying to "save my own life" from embarrassment and inconvenience, and to no longer fear man more than God. I repented of my faithlessness and I resolved to both seek and follow the inspiration that is to be had through the Holy Ghost, both while I was serving as a missionary and from that point onward. This does not mean I was suddenly perfect. I was still a young man beset by many of the challenges and imperfections that all young men are subject too. But my resolve to forget myself, to truly lose myself, to not fear men more than God, and to follow the Spirit as I served the Lord and my fellow man was resolute.

To live a life worth losing in the service of the Lord means to lay aside worldly values and cares and to take up our cross and follow Him. It means that we repent, follow the commandments, and deny ourselves of all ungodliness. It means that we trust in our Heavenly Father, that he knows our needs and will care for us if we follow His counsel and do His will. It means that we resolve to learn to listen to the quiet promptings of the Holy Spirit and to follow the personal revelation we receive via that divine conduit. It means that we cannot fear men more than God, and that we consecrate our time, our talents, and our treasures in building up the Kingdom of God on Earth. To live a life worth losing means that we place our Heavenly Father first and that we place our implicit trust in Him as we seek to do His will.

As my wife did in her introduction, I would like to express my gratitude for the faithful and selfless service that is rendered to the prophetic mission of this great institution by faculty, staff, and administrators who daily give consecrated service to the Savior by serving their fellow man. Many of them have training, experience, and qualifications that far exceed what one would typically find at an institution of this size. If you ask them, they will tell you that they felt divinely called to come here, and therefore they lay aside other much more lucrative and prestigious opportunities to heed that call. This sacrifice is too often unnoticed and unappreciated, but that is not what they are after. Rather, they have willingly chosen to forget themselves, and to lose themselves in selfless service to the Lord and the gospel.

To you students who will one day graduate from Brigham Young University-Hawaii, I offer a challenge: that if you have not already done so, resolve today that you will strive to forget yourself and to live a life worth losing. Troublesome times are to be visited upon this Earth and it will take a strong testimony of the gospel to resist the ways of the world, including the temptation to try to save our lives by faithlessly seeking for worldly riches or for a life of ease that is devoid of higher purpose. It is not for me to say what your lives will bring, but I promise you that in following the Savior's admonition to take up your cross and follow him, and by resolving to lose yourself in His service, and in the service of the gospel and your fellow man, it is then that you will truly find yourself, and that your life and the lives of those who are dear to you will be saved.

I testify to you that God lives, and that He is mindful of you. I testify that He can make so much more of your life than you can ever do on your own. I testify that Jesus is the Christ, the savior of the world, and that his gospel has been restored in its fullness in our day through the prophet Joseph Smith. I testify that Thomas S. Monson is a prophet of God and that this institution is led by prophets and apostles who would seek to have us use the resources placed at our disposal to accomplish the great mission that was foreseen at its founding, even the training of men and women who cannot be bought or sold, genuine gold, who will wisely and selflessly work towards the establishment of peace internationally. This is my witness in the name of Jesus Christ. Amen.

# APPENDIX C:
## GROUP DISCUSSION QUESTIONS

It is my hope that the story you've just read has given you the kind of hope my journey has given me. To help you sort through your own experiences, I've provided a few questions to ponder and discuss.

*Stay safe,*
*Diana Hubner, The Tire Mom*

1. Clayton's death was the biggest loss of my life; you may have experienced a big loss as well. Other kinds of loss can be almost as devastating—from the end of a job to a hit to your health. I know how much it helps to talk about those losses. Will you share yours with the group?

2. Have you found any kind of purpose in the grief you've endured? It doesn't have to be as ambitious as gifting tires in fifty states. Anything positive that arises from grief counts.

3. In the grieving process, what stage has been the most difficult? The five stages of grief are denial, anger, bargaining, depression, and acceptance.

4. Grief and loss often leave us questioning who we are. Has that been your experience? What have you learned about yourself in the process of healing?

5. As you've seen, I like to use metaphors to express my inner processes—tile floors, mountains, drops of healing, ocean waves. What images have helped you come to terms with a loss and the subsequent healing?

6. I talk about the mountains I've had to climb or will climb—the tire journey, the book, and whatever approach I take to spreading the tire safety word. What mountains have formed themselves in your path as you've healed from loss? Will you climb them?

7. I mention several traditions and practices we had as a family that taught our kids valuable lessons and helped us grow closer. A friend who is now a widow once told me that the best advice she ever got was "to make good memories together." What are ideas you have for deliberately creating good memories with people close to you? How can those memories later help with the healing process?

8. One of the biggest lessons I had to learn was to receive blessings gratefully. Where are you in that area? Can you appreciate the blessings coming your way even in the midst of sorrow?

9. I learned through visiting memorials that it is helpful to honor our lost loved ones in some concrete way. What have you done or could you do to mark the legacy someone has left?

10. Which aspects of tire safety were you aware of before you read this book, and which ones were new to you? How will you share your new knowledge with friends and family?

11. Have you checked your tires lately?

## U.S. STATES WITH ANNUAL VEHICLE SAFETY INSPECTIONS

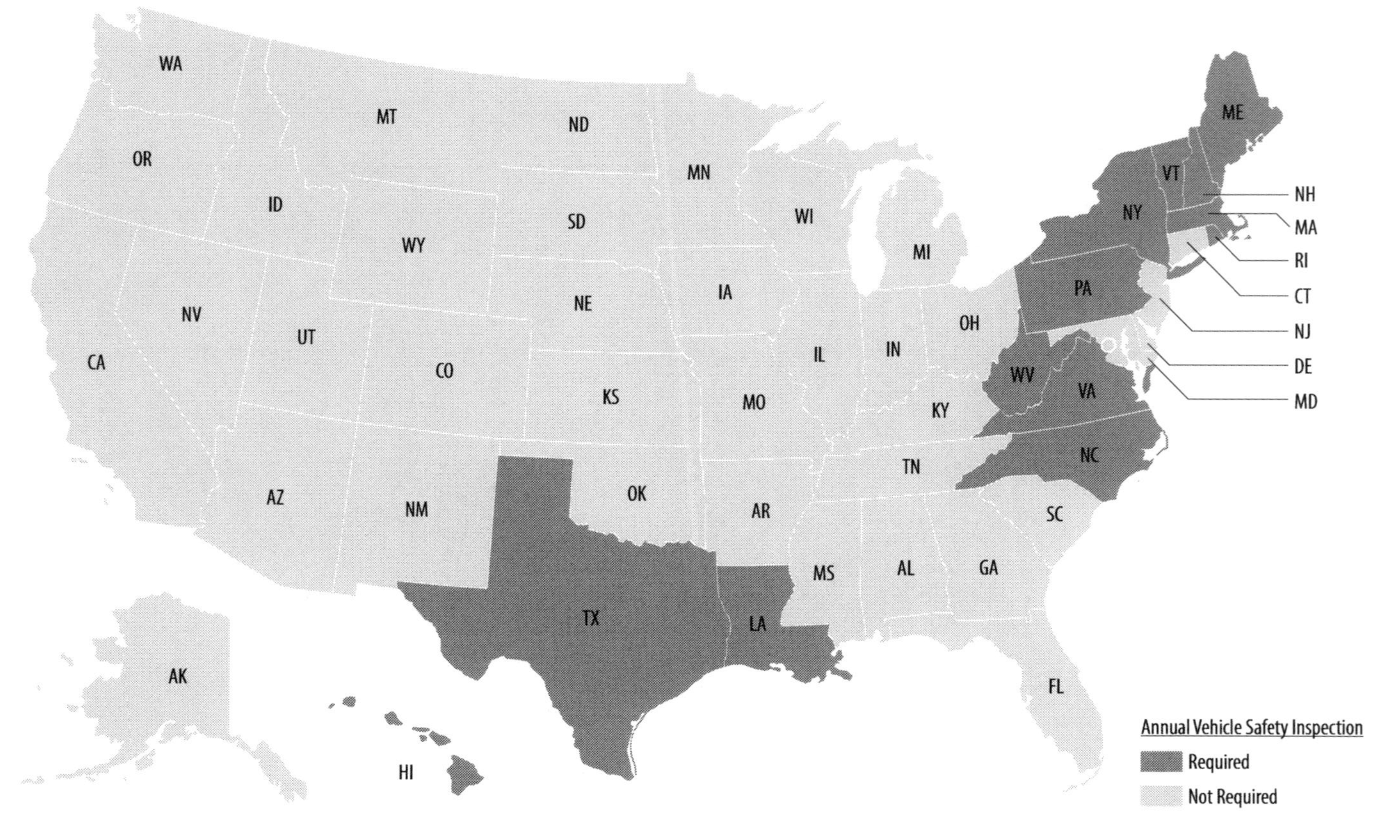

# APPENDIX D:

## ANNUAL VEHICLE SAFETY INSPECTIONS

The map to the left shows the thirteen U.S. states with annual safety inspections.

The following websites contain information about vehicle safety inspections in each of the fifty U.S. states. All of the links were active as of September 2019.

NO = no annual inspection

YES = annual inspection required

Although some of the states do not require annual inspections, they may require inspections every two years, or other types of inspection such as upon the transfer of ownership of a vehicle.

AL: NO - https://www.dontwaitlong.com/alabama-vehicle-inspection-laws/

AK: NO - http://doa.alaska.gov/dmv/reg/home.htm

AZ: NO - https://azdot.gov/motor-vehicles/vehicle-services

AR: NO - https://www.dmv.org/ar-arkansas/smog-check.php

CA: NO - https://www.dmv.ca.gov/portal/dmv/?1dmy&urile=wcm:path:/dmv_content_en/dmv/forms/ol/ol221a

CO: NO - https://www.colorado.gov/pacific/dmv/site-search?search_term=car+safety+inspections

CT: NO - https://portal.ct.gov/Services/Driving-and-Transportation/Inspections-and-Emissions-Testing

DE: NO - https://dmv.de.gov/VehicleServices/inspections/index.shtml?dc=v_equipment

FL: NO - https://www.flhsmv.gov/safety-center/vehicle-safety/

GA: NO - https://www.dmv.org/ga-georgia/smog-check.php

HI: YES - http://www.honolulu.gov/index.php/cms-csd-menu/site-csd-sitearticles/6440-faqs-about-reconstructed-vehicle-inspection.html

ID: NO - http://www.idahovip.org/faq.html

IL: NO - http://www.idot.illinois.gov/Assets/uploads/files/IDOT-Forms/TS/TS%203000.pdf

IN: NO - https://www.emissions.org/loc/indiana-emissions-testing/

IA: NO - https://iowadot.gov/search-results?q=vehicle%20safety%20inspection

KS: NO - https://www.douglascountyks.org/depts/treasurer/vehicle-inspections#Link-To-When-Vehicle-Inspections-Are-Required

KY: NO - https://drive.ky.gov/Motor-Vehicle-Licensing/Pages/Mandatory-Insurance.aspx

LA: YES - http://www.lsp.org/lse_form4.html

ME: YES - https://www.maine.gov/dps/msp/investigation-traffic/crash-investigations/mv-inspections

MD: NO - http://www.mva.maryland.gov/about-mva/info/58000ASE/58000-01T.htm#appendixA

MA: YES - https://www.mass.gov/service-details/vehicle-inspections

MI: NO - https://www.emissions.org/loc/michigan-emissions-testing/

MN: NO - https://dps.mn.gov/divisions/msp/commercial-vehicles/Pages/mandatory-inspection-program-mip.aspx

MS: NO - https://www.dps.ms.gov/search/node?keys=vehicle+safety+inspection

MO: NO - https://dor.mo.gov/motorv/help.php

MT: NO - https://dojmt.gov/driving/vehicle-identification-number-vin-inspections/

NE: NO - https://www.emissions.org/loc/nebraska-emissions-testing/

NV: NO - https://dmvnv.com/nvregreq.htm

NH: YES - https://www.nh.gov/safety/divisions/dmv/registration/inspections-emissions/index.htm

NJ: NO - https://www.state.nj.us/mvc/inspection/aboutinsp.htm

NM: NO - http://www.mvd.newmexico.gov/register-your-vehicle.aspx

NC: YES - https://www.ncdot.gov/dmv/title-registration/emissions-safety/Pages/safety-inspections.aspx

NC: YES - https://www.ncdot.gov/dmv/title-registration/emissions-safety/Pages/safety-inspections.aspx

ND: NO - https://www.emissions.org/loc/north-dakota-emissions-testing/

OH: NO - https://www.dmv.org/oh-ohio/smog-check.php

OK: NO - https://www.ok.gov/dps/Administrative_Rules/Inspection_and_Equipment_for_Motor_Vehicles/Annual_Motor_Vehicle_Inspection_and_Emission_Anti-Tampering_Inspection_Records_and_Reports/

OR: NO - https://www.oregon.gov/deq/Vehicle-Inspection/Pages/Prepare-for-the-Test.aspx

PA: YES - https://www.dmv.pa.gov/VEHICLE-SERVICES/Inspection-Information/Safety-Inspection-Program/Pages/default.aspx

RI: YE S- https://www.riinspection.org/Pages/FAQ.aspx?ID=generalfaq

SC: NO - https://www.postandcourier.com/news/how-are-sc-cars-faring-over-years-after-doing-away/article_4e5cf18c-968c-11e9-a797-1363877a1f6d.html

SD: NO - https://www.dmv.org/ne-nebraska/smog-check.php

TN: NO- https://www.williamsoncounty-tn.gov/1351/TN-Vehicle-Inspection-Program-Emissions

TX: Yes- https://www.dps.texas.gov/rsd/vi/inspection/inspectioncriteria.aspx

UT: NO - https://site.utah.gov/dps-highway/wp-content/uploads/sites/21/2017/12/Keepmyvehiclesafeandlegal.pdf

VT: YES - https://dec.vermont.gov/air-quality/mobile-sources/vehicle-inspections

VA: YES - https://www.vsp.virginia.gov/Safety.shtm#InspectionProgram

WA: NO - https://www.emissions.org/loc/washington-emissions-testing/

WV: YES - https://transportation.wv.gov/DMV/Vehicle-Services/Pages/Vehicle-Inspection.aspx

WI: NO - https://wisconsindot.gov/Pages/dmv/vehicles/rnew-plts/emissiontest.aspx

WY: NO - http://www.dot.state.wy.us/home/search.html

# APPENDIX E:

## LETMAP

**Let the Map**

# L

**Lug Nuts:**
Re-torque lug nuts
50-100 miles after installing
or rotating tires.

# E

**Examine Tires:**
Recommendations say
to check your tires
once a month.

# T

**Tread:**
States have different
tread depth requirements.
Know your state. Be safe.

**Mileage:**
Tire mileage warranties
differ. Know your mileage.

# M

**Age:**
Check your Tire Halo.
First two numbers = Week
Last two numbers = Year

# A

**Pressure:**
Find the recommended
pressure inside driver's door.
Check once a month.

**guide you!**

# LETMAP

## SUMMARY

**Lug Nuts** – Lug nuts keep your tire on your car. However, if they are too loose, your tire may come off while you are driving; if they are too tight, you may not be able to remove the tire easily when needed, such as when you get a flat. After you get new tires and after you get your tires rotated, the store or garage will usually ask you to return after you've driven 50-100 miles to get the wheels re-torqued, which ensures that the lugs nuts are tightened to the correct degree. This service is usually free, so take advantage of it.

**Examination** – Examination is an essential part of tire maintenance. Even if the other aspects of tire safety are adhered to, thorough examination might reveal an issue that doesn't relate to the other categories of LETMAP, for instance deformations.

**Tread** – Tread helps your tire grip the road and affects the handling of your vehicle. Most new tires come with tread that is approximately 10 32nds of an inch deep (10/32"). The U.S. Department of Transportation recommends that once the tread on your tires reaches 2/32", the tires should be replaced (in some states this is required by law). A convenient time to check your tread depth is when you are doing your monthly tire pressure check. The "penny test" is a common method, but there are other ways. For remaining questions, talk to the experts!

**Mileage & Warranty** – Almost every type of tire comes with a warranty that covers the tire for a specific number of years or until the tire has between 20,000 and 100,000 miles on it, depending on the type of tire. This is essentially a guarantee that you will get a certain amount of use out of the tire. Thus, it is important to record and keep track of the mileage of your tires.

**Age** – As I've emphasized in this book, it is dangerous to drive on old tires. Several automobile manufacturers warn drivers to replace vehicle tires after six years. You can calculate the age of your tire by finding the manufacture date inside the Tire Halo on the tire's sidewall. For example, the number in the halo might be 25/19. This means that the tire was made in the twenty-fifth week of the year 2019. Identify the manufacture dates of all of the tires on your car and write them down. For remaining questions, talk to the experts.

**Pressure** – A car's recommended tire pressure can usually be found on a sticker inside the driver's door or in the owner's manual. The sidewall of the tire lists the maximum pressure that the tire can be inflated to, which is a different number than the recommended pressure; however, it is not optimally efficient or safe to fill the tire to the maximum pressure. Check your tires' pressure at least once a month and keep them properly inflated. Don't forget to check the spare!

*Please* read and study this section. The knowledge it contains could save your life and the lives of those you love. Feel free to photocopy it and keep it in your glove box. All you need to remember is to: **LET the MAP guide your travels.**

# APPENDIX F:

| | AL | AK | AZ | AR | CA | CO | CT | DE | FL | GA | HI | ID | IL | IN | IA | KS | KY | LA | ME | MD | MA | MI | MN | MS | MO |
|---|---|---|---|---|---|---|---|---|---|---|---|---|---|---|---|---|---|---|---|---|---|---|---|---|---|
| **L** | | | – | | | | | | | | – | | | | | | | | – | | | | | | |
| **E** | X | X | X | X | X | X | X | X | X | X | X | – | – | X | X | X | X | X | X | – | X | – | X | – | X |
| **T** | – | X | X | X | X | X | X | X | – | X | X | – | – | X | X | X | X | X | X | – | X | – | X | – | X |
| **M** | | | | | | | | | | | | | | | | | | | | | | | | | |
| **A** | | | | | | | | | | – | | | | | | | | | | | | | | | |
| **P** | – | X | X | X | X | X | X | X | – | X | X | – | | X | X | X | X | X | X | | X | – | X | – | X |

| | MT | NE | NV | NH | NJ | NM | NY | NC | ND | OH | OK | OR | PA | RI | SC | SD | TN | TX | UT | VT | VA | WA | WV | WI | WY |
|---|---|---|---|---|---|---|---|---|---|---|---|---|---|---|---|---|---|---|---|---|---|---|---|---|---|
| **L** | | | | – | | | | | | – | – | | – | | | | | | | | | | | | |
| **E** | X | X | X | X | X | – | X | X | X | – | – | – | X | X | X | X | X | – | – | X | X | X | X | X | X |
| **T** | X | X | X | – | X | – | X | X | X | – | – | – | X | X | X | X | X | – | – | X | X | X | X | X | X |
| **M** | | | | | | | | | | | | | | | | | | | | | | | | | |
| **A** | | | | | | | | | | | | | | | | | | | | | | | | | |
| **P** | X | X | X | – | X | – | X | X | X | – | – | | X | X | X | X | X | – | – | X | X | X | X | X | X |

**DMV Driver Manual vs. LETMAP**

X Topic Covered

– Topic Mentioned

Blank Topic Not Covered

# APPENDIX G:

| | Model | Make | Year | Mileage | Tread Depth |
|---|---|---|---|---|---|
| **Car** | | | | | |
| **Tire** | | | | | |

| Front Left Tire | | LET the MAP guide you! | | Front Right Tire | |
|---|---|---|---|---|---|
| *Purchase Date* | *Halo Number* | | | *Purchase Date* | *Halo Number* |
| **Replacement** | | | | **Replacement** | |
| *Purchase Date* | *Halo Number* | | | *Purchase Date* | *Halo Number* |
| **Rear Left Tire** | | **Spare Tire** | | **Rear Right Tire** | |
| *Purchase Date* | *Halo Number* | *Purchase Date* | *Halo Number* | *Purchase Date* | *Halo Number* |
| **Replacement** | | **Replacement** | | **Replacement** | |
| *Purchase Date* | *Halo Number* | *Purchase Date* | *Halo Number* | *Purchase Date* | *Halo Number* |

# ABOUT DIANA HUBNER

Diana W. Hubner was an ordinary stay-at-home mother for twenty-seven years until Father's Day 2012 when her husband, Clayton, was killed in a car accident caused by tire tread separation. This incident inspired her to found The Tire Mom, LLC, a company whose mission is to make the USA a safer place by educating people on how to read the manufacture date on their tires.

Diana has lived in thirteen different states and three foreign countries, and has called a staggering thirty-five different places home throughout her life. As an empty nester, Diana loves snuggling with her three dogs as she watches her favorite movie series, *The Lord of the Rings,* for the five millionth time.

# ABOUT NANCY RUE

Nancy Rue is an American Christian novelist, writing for tweens and adults. She is known for the *Lily* series of novels featuring twelve-year-old Lily Robbins. She is also known for the *Sophie* series.

Made in the USA
Columbia, SC
12 March 2020

88996853R00133